MEASURING CUSTOMER SATISFACTION: HOT BUTTONS AND OTHER MEASUREMENT ISSUES

MEASURING CUSTOMER SATISFACTION:
HOT BUTTONS AND OTHER MEASUREMENT ISSUES

JAMES H. MYERS, PH.D.
The Drucker School
Claremont Graduate University

American Marketing Association
Chicago, Illinois

Library of Congress Cataloging-in-Publication Data

Myers, James H.
Measuring customer satisfaction : hot buttons and other
    measurement issues / James H. Myers.
    p. cm.
Includes bibliographical references and index.
ISBN 0-87757-276-3 (hardcover)
    1. Consumer satisfaction—United States—Evaluation.
I. Title.
HF5415.335.M93   1999   99-32740
658.8'12'072—dc21   CIP

Published by American Marketing Association
311 S. Wacker Dr., Ste. 5800
Chicago, IL 60606 USA

Francesca VanGorp Cooley, Editor
Elisabeth Nevins, Copy Editor
Natalie Bielinski, Editorial Project Assistant
Mary Loye, Compositor

Designed by Nicole Szymanski

Manufactured in the United States of America

TABLE OF CONTENTS

FOREWORD

Customer satisfaction emerged as an area for serious study approximately 30 years ago. I, along with most U.S. business firms, largely ignored the early studies and concepts as they kept appearing in the marketing and business literature. There was a tendency for all of us to say, "I know all about the importance of keeping customers happy and satisfied. I don't need to be reminded."

But eventually, the sheer volume of articles, papers, and programs compelled our attention to the customer satisfaction movement and led to the realization that this topic was for real and that it was "onto something." But why was satisfying the customer suddenly so important? After all, a customer orientation was the cornerstone of the Marketing Concept that had been so influential in American business since the 1950s. Wasn't this enough? Apparently not, in too many companies. (In Chapter 1, I discuss my view of the reasons for the decline of interest in the Marketing Concept and the emergence of the customer satisfaction movement.)

However, the more I read the customer satisfaction literature, the more concerned I became about the methodologies used in the measurement of satisfaction. These methods ranged from overly sophisticated experiments by academics to overly simplistic surveys conducted by many market research firms. All of these disparate efforts seemed to have hardly any common ground. I think it safe to say that, even today, there is no generally accepted paradigm for the measurement of customer satisfaction. To many companies, it is no different than basic market research surveys. However, a few companies and academics have made a serious effort to develop more sophisticated survey instruments that are much more appropriate for the accurate measurement of customer satisfaction.

The measurement program is the foundation on which any serious customer satisfaction effort rests. If it is weak, the entire program is compromised. Therefore, it is worth the extra time to get the measurements right.

This book is based on the proposition that customer satisfaction measurement (CSM) requirements differ in some important ways from those of basic market research surveys. These differences are discussed throughout the book. In spite of these differences, the general framework and principles for market surveys still apply. I think of successful satisfaction measurement as a market research "cake" with a customer satisfaction "frosting." Although the cake alone is adequate, an excellent frosting does much to enhance the flavor and, thus, the effectiveness of the entire package. I hope that some of the ideas in this book will improve the effectiveness of customer satisfaction programs by suggesting modifications in basic market research survey methods and techniques that will result in more accurate and useful measurements.

Hot Buttons

One problem in every measurement program is determining the relative importance of the attributes on which customers and others rate the company and perhaps competitors as well. Important attributes are the "hot buttons" on which companies need to concentrate their efforts and resources. This is obvious. What is not obvious is the difficulty and confusion involved in this task, because *different methods used to measure attribute importance often produce different results*. How does one know which method or methods to use? Which is the most accurate?

This book describes approximately a dozen different methods and techniques that have been used to measure attribute importance in a wide variety of settings. These methods have been classified arbitrarily into 2 categories: direct and indirect. Direct methods are transparent in the sense that respondents know they are being asked to indicate the importance of each attribute in one way or another. Indirect methods infer or derive attribute importance from responses to structured questions or from tasks that are probably opaque to respondents. Both approaches are legitimate, but they often yield different results.

All these techniques are described, illustrated, and evaluated briefly across several chapters. Then, recommendations are made as to which of these are likely to be most effective in several circumstances. It is always wise to estimate attribute importance in more than one way, preferably with one direct and one indirect technique. Results then can be compared graphically, and attributes that represent a firm's "cost of entry" can be identified. These are attributes that *must* be present in a product or service offering because they are expected by customers, but a company gets little or no credit for them because every competitor also has them. I discuss this in Chapter 6.

Outline of Book

Chapters 1 and 2 set the stage by discussing the current status of CSM programs in the United States. They also provide an overview of 4 major types of rating scales that can be used to measure satisfaction, along with types and sources of attributes to be rated by customers and perhaps by competitors' customers.

Chapters 3 through 5 describe and illustrate the various techniques for measuring the relative importance of attributes. Direct methods are discussed in Chapter 3, and indirect methods in Chapters 4 and 5. Chapter 6 presents what little evidence is available that compares results by applying 2 or more methods to survey responses from the same persons at the same point in time. Then, a method for plotting results from any 2 methods, preferably one direct and one indirect, is presented and illustrated. This leads directly to the identification of "cost of entry" attributes.

Chapter 7 contains a review of some basic principles of good performance rating scales. These principles have been developed during many decades by investigators in both market research and public opinion polling. This chapter also presents some results from studies conducted by Bellcore to evaluate the effectiveness of several alternative performance rating scale formats. Several recommendations are made for selecting an appropriate scale for different satisfaction measurement scenarios and objectives.

Chapter 8 introduces the idea of using *comparison standards* in rating scale construction. There are 2 general types of such scales: single expectations/performance and dual expectations/performance. Each of these is illustrated. Then, I present a comparison of results from a single expectations/performance scale versus a simple performance rating scale, with the same attributes and respondents at the same point in time. Implications for CSM are suggested.

Chapter 9 discusses several other measurement issues, including strategic breakpoints, market damage assessment, "moving the needle," and the reliability and validity of rating scale measurement. Chapter 10 presents several different approaches to developing a customer satisfaction index and makes some recommendations for constructing an appropriate one. Finally, Chapter 11 discusses several aspects of the overall design and the administration of an effective customer satisfaction program.

ACKNOWLEDGMENTS

I especially want to thank Arne Haug and Gary Mullet for their careful and thoughtful reviews of previous drafts of this book. Arne is the principal of Haug International Inc., a Los Angeles–based firm that specializes in marketing research, market strategy formulation, and CSM. He read every page of the draft and offered a great many suggestions about format and specific content, primarily from a managerial perspective. It was while I was working on customer satisfaction studies for his clients that I learned many of the ideas and principles presented in this book.

Gary Mullet, Ph.D., is the principal of Gary Mullet Associates Inc., a marketing research and statistical consulting firm in Atlanta. Gary is professionally trained in high-technology statistical analysis and has many years of experience in analyzing data from market and customer satisfaction surveys. He carefully reviewed the entire manuscript from a technical perspective and offered many suggestions and clarifications, all of which are incorporated. These 2 reviewers greatly improved the contents of this book. Any errors of either commission or omission are mine alone.

Finally, I want to thank Ani Missakian, who typed the entire manuscript in final form and offered occasional editorial suggestions. A manuscript of this size sometimes requires major revisions and often can benefit from careful attention to small details. Ani is very good at both of these tasks, and this made my own job easier. A good book is really a team effort, and I had a first-rate support group.

CHAPTER 1

ORIGINS AND CURRENT STATUS

Serious interest in "customer satisfaction," as a more or less formal operating philosophy, is recent in U.S. businesses. It began circa 1990, when several factors converged to produce an unusually trying business climate: an economic recession, hypercompetition from both domestic and foreign firms, and shrinkage in many global markets. Of particular concern to American business firms was the continuing loss of local business to foreign competitors. In many industries, foreign companies showed they were better able to understand and supply U.S. customers than were American companies.

In response, many business firms greatly increased their emphasis on programs designed to understand their customers better, increase their ability to satisfy customer needs, improve product and/or service quality, and, thus, increase their ability to succeed in highly competitive markets. These programs have included

- • • Total Quality Management (TQM)/Quality Function Deployment,
- • • Customer Satisfaction/Dissatisfaction,

• • • Relationship Marketing, and
• • • Value Propositions/Value Delivery Systems.

All of these have the general objective of improving the quality and desirability of companies' product and/or service offerings and making firms more responsive to market needs and desires. Each movement has been formalized in one way or another through books, conferences, periodical journals, or even its own professional associations. These efforts have had a major impact on the ability of organizations of all types to satisfy customer needs and thereby to compete more effectively. In this book, we focus only on *customer satisfaction*, arguably the ultimate objective of all these movements, with primary emphasis on *measurement issues* of various kinds. Measuring customer satisfaction accurately and usefully is a great deal more difficult than it seems.

This chapter presents:

• • • A brief historical overview of the customer satisfaction movement and its relationship to the Marketing Concept,
• • • The current status of selected aspects of customer satisfaction measurement (CSM) programs,
• • • The recommended steps for developing effective measuring instruments, and
• • • The 4 major types of satisfaction rating scales.

CUSTOMER ORIENTATION: A BRIEF HISTORY

The early 1990s was not the first time American business firms in the aggregate had made serious and sustained efforts to focus on customers. Perhaps the first formal industrywide initiative of this kind began circa 1950, when General Electric introduced what it called the "Marketing Concept" (Kotler 1997, p. 19; Webster 1997, p. 44). At the heart of this proposal was the belief that the customer should be at the center of planning activities and that all the resources of the firm should be organized around serving customer needs. This set off a flurry of activity among business firms of all types aimed at developing internal marketing organizations and conducting marketing research to determine what customers really wanted. The objective was nothing less than to transform companies from mere production operations into customer-oriented, customer-satisfying organizations.

The Marketing Concept rested on several basic propositions:

1. Having a customer orientation,
2. Establishing a chief marketing executive with high corporate status,

3. Establishing marketing staff functions (e.g., marketing research, product management, new product planning),
4. Integrating all marketing functions (e.g., advertising, personal selling, sales promotion, marketing staff functions) under the direction of the chief marketing executive, and
5. Emphasizing profits rather than volume of sales.

Many of these propositions were foreign to most U.S. business firms in the early 1950s. The 1950s and 1960s were a time of rather painful transition for many companies, even those that had a genuine interest in becoming more customer oriented.

The Marketing Concept certainly had a real impact in making many business firms, and other types of organizations, much more responsive to customer needs. Yet, we could argue that if it had succeeded as it should have, there would have been no need for the customer satisfaction movement (as well as TQM and other movements) during the late 1980s and up to the present. Companies that were customer oriented, according to the Marketing Concept, should have been satisfying customer needs at least adequately. Of course, some business firms and other organizations did this very effectively; however, many others did not. As early as 1985, Jack Welsh, Chief Executive Officer (CEO) of General Electric (the company that introduced the Marketing Concept) was quoted as saying, "Where is marketing now that we need it?"

What Went Wrong with the Marketing Concept?

In my opinion, there were three major reasons the Marketing Concept did not deliver all it promised. The first was that the heavy emphasis on developing an internal marketing organization that would ensure a customer orientation resulted in too many companies unintentionally putting the focus on the *marketing department* or *function* rather than on the *customer*. In effect, marketing people would say to other functional areas within the firm, "Listen to us. We will tell you what customers want. Then we'll coordinate all functional areas in the firm to see that customers get what they want." In most companies, all customer research was either performed or coordinated by the marketing research function, thus lending credibility to these claims. Many marketing departments made a major effort to acquire and control all customer-related information within the firm and then to develop marketing plans designed to coordinate all the functional areas to satisfy customer needs at a profit.

However, many marketing specialists within some firms were not capable of living up to these claims and objectives. They had neither the training nor the experience required. There is also the question of whether *any* marketing department, by itself, can find out everything the entire company needs to know about satisfying customer needs.

This philosophy also caused resentment toward marketing among other functions in the firm, because the marketing department proposed taking away part of the influence that traditionally had resided elsewhere in the firm (e.g., technology labs, production or operations, finance). The net result was that, somewhere along the line, it became necessary to shift the emphasis *away* from the marketing function and *onto the customer directly*. The customer satisfaction movement has been one very effective way of doing this for many business firms and other types of organizations.

A second problem with the Marketing Concept was that the traditional role of marketing had concentrated more on acquiring *new* customers than on retaining and satisfying *existing* customers. It was only after research in several companies demonstrated that the cost of acquiring a new customer was approximately *5 times* the cost of retaining an existing one that top management in many companies became aware of the leveraging effect of keeping existing customers happy. Unfortunately, the customer orientation plank of the Marketing Concept platform had a tendency to focus more on company promotion efforts to gain new customers than on fulfilling the needs of present customers better than competitors could.

A third problem with the Marketing Concept was that it usually did not include any requirements for systematic, continuous, and objective *tracking* that would monitor the satisfaction of existing customers in terms of how well their various needs were being met. Marketing research tended to focus on specific decisions or plans the marketing department needed to obtain new customers, not on monitoring the satisfaction of existing customers, which might serve as a basis for ongoing improvement efforts that involved all parts of the firm. Many business firms were not able to manage customer satisfaction because many managers believed that "if you can't measure it, you can't manage it."

Enter Customer Satisfaction

As long as business conditions were reasonably good in the United States, the Marketing Concept represented a major improvement over the more traditional forms of organization and operation. It brought a greater focus on the customer in many firms and provided one means of improving the integration of the various functional areas to serve customer needs better. But it was not enough. As competition became more intense in the late 1980s, top management in many companies became convinced that it needed a better means of staying in touch with customers as a whole, of knowing how well its organization was satisfying the needs of those customers, and of spotting weaknesses before they became major problems.

The customer satisfaction movement offered one good way to do this. It provided a scorecard that was easily understood, without a lot of complex statistical manipulation. It also represented the "voice of the customer" directly and on an ongoing basis. Therefore, it provided measurements that could inform *all parts* of the organization about customer perceptions and evaluations. For perhaps the first time in many companies, the customer finally had arrived in the executive suite (and even in some boardrooms) in a systematic, objective way that was easy to understand and hard to ignore. All of these alterations triggered major changes in many business firms and other types of organizations, changes that were designed to increase satisfaction and, more important, *retention* among existing customers. Today, it is common to see references to customer satisfaction in annual reports to shareholders of both consumer and business-to-business companies.

Customer satisfaction has arrived not only in business firms of all types, but also in that bureaucratic maze known as the U.S. Government. Part of the text of an Executive Order (#12862, *Fed. Reg.*, September 11, 1993), signed by President Clinton in 1993, states:

> Putting people first means ensuring that the Federal Government provides the highest quality service possible to the American people. Public officials must embark upon a revolution within the Federal Government to change the way it does business. This will require continual reform of the executive branch's management practices and operations to provide service to the public that matches or exceeds the best service available in the private sector.
>
> NOW, THEREFORE, to establish and implement customer service standards to guide the operations of the executive branch, and by the authority vested in me as President by the Constitution and the laws of the United States, it is hereby ordered:
>
> **Section 1.** *Customer Service Standards.* In order to carry out the principles of the National Performance Review, the Federal Government must be customer-driven. The standard of quality for services provided to the public shall be: Customer service equal to the best in business. For the purposes of this order, "customer" shall mean an individual or entity who is directly served by a department or agency. "Best in business" shall mean the highest quality of service delivered to customers by private organizations providing a comparable or analogous service.

All executive departments and agencies (hereinafter referred to collective-ly as "agency" or "agencies") that provide significant services directly to the public shall provide those services in a manner that seeks to meet the customer service standard established herein and shall take the following actions:

(a) identify the customers who are, or should be, served by the agency;
(b) survey customers to determine the kind and quality of services they want and their level of satisfaction with existing services;
(c) post service standards and measure results against them;
(d) benchmark customer service performance against the best in business;
(e) survey front-line employees on barriers to, and ideas for, matching the best in business;
(f) provide customers with choices in both the sources of service and the means of delivery;
(g) make information, services, and complaint systems easily accessible; and
(h) provide means to address customer complaints.

Section 2. *Report on Customer Service Surveys.* By March 8, 1994, each agency subject to this order shall report on its customer surveys to the President. As information about customer satisfaction becomes available, each agency shall use that information in judging the performance of agency management and in making resource allocations.

Many cynics will smile in reading this order. They will doubt that a bureaucracy as vast as this one can be ordered to make such major changes in operating philosophies and practices. It remains to be seen how well the various agencies and departments will respond. Judging from experience, some probably will make meaningful progress, and others will change very little.

CURRENT STATUS OF CUSTOMER SATISFACTION PROGRAMS

Although it would be nice to know approximately what percentage of U.S. business firms have formal customer satisfaction programs in place, this figure would be nearly impossible to determine. Probably only medium-sized or larger companies would have the resources to staff such a program and/or fund ongoing customer research for the purpose of monitoring satisfaction. Also, many firms, large and small, easily could say they have a customer satisfaction "program" when in fact their efforts are largely informal, unstaffed, uncoordinated, without a meaningful budget, and/or not monitored on a regular basis.

(For years, many companies have measured their corporate image using tracking studies of customer perceptions and evaluations. Some continue to do so, and this activity has served as a surrogate for a CSM program.)

Instead, let us review the results of a recent survey conducted by Mentzer, Bienstock, and Kahn (1995) of 124 business firms, mostly in the United States. Approximately half of these firms had sales between $100 million and $10 billion, and 63% had more than 1000 employees. More than half the respondents were managers or directors. Thus, "the results are largely from managers/directors in larger corporations in the United States that market a wide range of products/services to other companies and final consumers" (p. 44). The questionnaire covered several aspects of CSM programs, some of which are presented here.

Executing the Program

Figure 1.1 shows the resources used to conduct a CSM program. More than 80% of the companies responding use their own staff employees (often the marketing research department) to establish CSM programs, more than 60% also use external consultants, more than 50% use their own customers, and more than 20% use competitors'

▼**FIGURE 1.1 RESOURCES USED TO ESTABLISH PROGRAM**

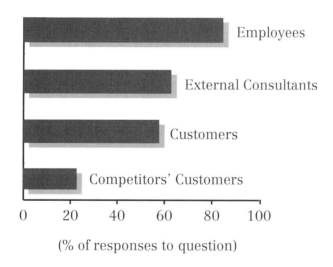

(% of responses to question)

Source: Mentzer, John T., Carol C. Bienstock, and Kenneth B. Kahn (1995), "Benchmarking Satisfaction," *Marketing Management*, 4 (Summer), 41–46.

customers. Marketing is the department that most frequently partici-pates in the design and implementation of CSM (78% of companies), with the sales department ranking next (50%). Figure 1.2 shows budg-et allocations for customer satisfaction programs. Interestingly, 16% of the firms spend $500,000 or more, another 31% spend $100,000 to $500,000, and 18% budget nothing!

The choice of attributes to be rated by customers (and noncus-tomers, if possible) is of critical importance to a CSM program. Omis-sion of important attributes can defeat the entire purpose of the pro-gram, whereas redundancy can increase both respondent fatigue and survey costs. Figure 1.3 shows that most companies (nearly 60%) ob-tain their measurement questions from focus groups, followed by management consultants, company management, employee sugges-tions, and pretest surveys (all at approximately 50% of companies). Figure 1.4 shows the type of customer service model or theory on which rating scales are based: approximately 25% used the SERVQUAL model (rating performance in relation to previous expec-tations, see Chapter 8), whereas more than 40% do not indicate any specific model.

Thus, we see a wide variety of approaches and resource dollars committed to customer satisfaction programs among a rather large

▼FIGURE 1.2 BUDGET ALLOCATION TO CUSTOMER SATISFACTION PROGRAM

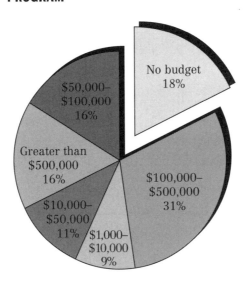

Source: Mentzer, John T., Carol C. Bienstock, and Kenneth B. Kahn (1995), "Bench-marking Satisfaction," *Marketing Management*, 4 (Summer), 41–46.

▼ FIGURE 1.3 HOW CUSTOMER SATISFACTION MEASUREMENT QUESTIONS ARE CHOSEN

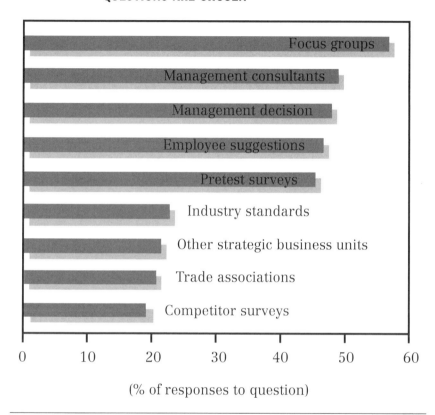

(% of responses to question)

Source: Mentzer, John T., Carol C. Bienstock, and Kenneth B. Kahn (1995), "Benchmarking Satisfaction," *Marketing Management*, 4 (Summer), 41–46.

sample of U.S. business firms. This is not surprising, and it tends to be true for any new program or initiative undertaken by a large number of companies.

IS THERE A PAYOFF?

Although the previously mentioned survey tells us something about how customer satisfaction surveys are conducted, it tells us nothing about the impact of these programs on the bottom lines. Does customer satisfaction pay off? Is it worth the effort? I do not know of any systematic survey of many large companies that could answer these questions across the board. Indeed, many companies have

▼ FIGURE 1.4 TYPE OF CUSTOMER SATISFACTION MODEL OR THEORY EMPLOYED

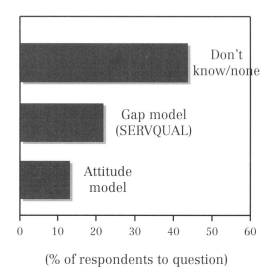

(% of respondents to question)

Source: Mentzer, John T., Carol C. Bienstock, and Kenneth B. Kahn (1995), "Bench-marking Satisfaction," *Marketing Management*, 4 (Summer), 41–46.

made little or no attempt to find answers. One exception is Toyota Motor Sales, U.S.A. This company has been among the leaders in systematic customer satisfaction programs and surveys. Results from one of their impact studies is shown in Figure 1.5. It shows selected financial comparisons between a group of its dealers with very high customer satisfaction ratings and another group with ratings near the bottom of all dealers. In this study, the top satisfaction dealers had an average of

• • • 46% higher net profit,
• • • 81% higher net profit as a percentage of sales,
• • • 67% higher net profit per employee,
• • • 10% lower new vehicle selling expense,
• • • 74% higher net profit as a percentage of gross profit,
• • • 43% less salesperson turnover, and
• • • 30% lower advertising costs per vehicle.

I have seen similar results in recent years from several other companies that have made the effort to measure the bottom-line impact of customer satisfaction programs. (Additional evidence on this topic can

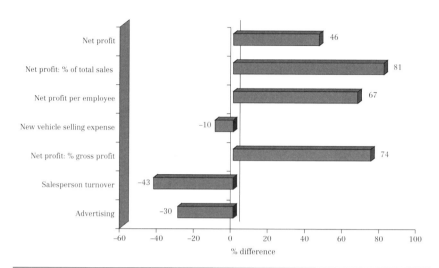

▼ FIGURE 1.5 FINANCIAL COMPARISON OF TOP VERSUS BOTTOM CUSTOMER SATISFACTION DEALERS

Reference: Toyota Motor Sales U.S.A.

be found in Chapter 11.) The Toyota study is particularly good because it compares high and low performing units at the same period of time, thereby eliminating the effects of such longitudinal factors as recessions and prosperity, competitive moves, and market changes of various kinds. *Every company should carry out studies of this kind on a continuing basis*, whenever possible. The evidence to date suggests that high customer satisfaction can indeed have positive effects on the bottom line.

CUSTOMER SATISFACTION MEASUREMENT

Although the remainder of this book is devoted to in-depth discussions of various measurement issues, it might be helpful, at this point, to present a brief overview of the major elements in a CSM program. This will serve as a framework for the more specific topics discussed in subsequent chapters. Some critical managerial issues, such as determining the objectives of the program, getting effective buy-in from employees and management, deciding exactly how results will be used or implemented, and establishing an internal custodian for the program with adequate staffing support, are discussed briefly in Chapter 11. These matters are not the primary focus of this book, but they are usually even more important than measurement issues!

Figure 1.6 shows 6 major questions that must be answered prior to establishing a measurement program. They address the following issues:

• • • What is the purpose(s) of the customer satisfaction program?
• • • Who will be surveyed?
• • • What tools are needed for measurement?
• • • Where do attributes come from?
• • • What type of measurement scale should be used?
• • • Should a Customer Satisfaction Index be constructed?

Each of these is discussed in this book.

Steps in Developing a Measuring Instrument

Every ongoing CSM program has, as one foundation, a structured questionnaire that is used at periodic intervals to secure evaluations from the company's customers, competitor's customers, former customers, and so forth. Because this questionnaire is the heart of most formal programs, it is extremely important that it be crafted with care at the outset. This is because customer survey results usually are stated in terms of *trends over time* and/or, more specifically, *changes* from one wave to another for the company as a whole or for specific divisions or offices. This means that changes cannot be made in attributes or rating scales from one wave to the next without affecting the results. The questionnaire should be constructed properly in the beginning so that frequent changes are not needed. Unfortunately, this is not always done, and then companies face the dilemma of continuing to use a poorly constructed questionnaire or changing to an improved one and losing continuity in some important aspects.

Constructing a good customer satisfaction questionnaire is not a "one-size-fits-all" task. Companies and industries differ widely in terms of objectives and characteristics. Nevertheless, it is possible to propose a framework that is likely to yield a reliable, valid, defensible measuring instrument for all constituents within the firm that are affected or interested. The steps shown in Figure 1.7 are recommended for companies that want the best possible preparation in constructing and using their ongoing customer satisfaction questionnaires. We discuss each step briefly in the following sections.

Statement of Objectives

At the outset, it is important to have a clear understanding of such factors as the following:

- • • What is the purpose of the customer satisfaction program?
- • • Who will be interviewed on an ongoing basis?
- • • How will results be used in the firm?

▼ FIGURE 1.6 CUSTOMER SATISFACTION MEASUREMENT PROGRAMS

1. What are the objectives?
   A. Retain more customers.
   B. Improve internal operations.
   C. Track changes over time.
   D. Make comparisons with leading competitors.
   E. Compensate employees.

2. Who will be surveyed?
   A. Customers.
   B. Competitor's customers.
   C. Former customers.
   D. Noncustomers.
   E. Employees (especially in sales).

3. What is needed for measurement?
   A. Performance attributes.
   B. Measurement scales.
   C. Summary/overall evaluations.

4. From where do attributes come?
   A. Focus groups of customers and/or former customers.
   B. Previous company research.
   C. Knowledgeable company personnel.

5. What type of measurement scale?
   A. Simple performance ratings.
   B. Simple satisfaction scale.
   C. Single performance/expectations scale.
   D. Dual performance/expectations scale.

6. Construct a Customer Satisfaction Index?
   A. Average overall satisfaction rating.
   B. Unweighted sum of attribute ratings.
   C. Weighted sum of attribute ratings:
      1. Judgment weights.
      2. Regression weights.

• • • Who needs to be involved in developing the program?
• • • Who will administer it on an ongoing basis?
• • • Are internal organization changes needed?
• • • Who will be rated by respondents within a customer firm?
• • • How will buy-in be achieved from employees who are affected?
• • • Will the program be outsourced or conducted internally?

▼ **FIGURE 1.7 SEQUENCE OF STEPS FOR CONSTRUCTING A MEASUREMENT INSTRUMENT**

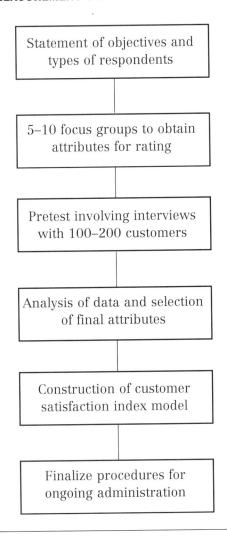

Statement of objectives and types of respondents

5–10 focus groups to obtain attributes for rating

Pretest involving interviews with 100–200 customers

Analysis of data and selection of final attributes

Construction of customer satisfaction index model

Finalize procedures for ongoing administration

Any or all of these can affect the construction of a suitable questionnaire, as well as the procedure for administering the program on an ongoing basis. Many of these points are managerial, not technical, and are beyond the scope of this book (see Naumann and Giel 1995).

Focus Groups

It is always best to conduct a series of focus groups to obtain a large number of satisfaction attributes directly from a sample of customers. This is discussed at greater length in Chapter 2.

Pretest

After a listing of 75 to 100 attributes has been obtained from the focus groups, these should be reduced to perhaps 15 to 25 for ongoing interviewing (though some companies use 30 to 40 and others use 70 to 80 to obtain enough specific information for clearer understanding and implementation). Customers cannot be expected to rate several dozen attributes in each interviewing wave, and it is not necessary that they do so. This reduction can be achieved on the basis of managerial judgment, but a far better way is by a *pretest* among a sample of perhaps 100 to 200 customers. Interviews should be conducted using the same method (mail, telephone, personal, Internet) that will be used on an ongoing basis. For these interviews, only performance ratings will be needed. The pretest is where the "hot buttons" should be identified.

Pretest Analysis

The resulting ratings can be analyzed in all of the following ways:

• • • *Frequency distributions* eliminate items that are so highly skewed (with all ratings at the top or bottom of the scale) that they fail to provide a sensitive measuring scale.
• • • *Factor analysis* eliminates attributes that excessively overlap with others and therefore are redundant.
• • • *Correlation analysis* eliminates items that do not show a meaningful relationship with overall satisfaction (i.e., $r \leq; .3 - .5$).
• • • *Relevance* eliminates items that the company can do nothing about, or does not want to change, or that can be better measured in other ways. This part requires management input.

These procedures are illustrated in Chapter 7.

Every item should be reviewed carefully in terms of all of these criteria, and perhaps others, which is not an easy task. Every group in the company that will be affected by customer satisfaction ratings should have a chance to comment. The goal is to arrive at a final set of perhaps 15 to 25 attributes that will provide a meaningful appraisal of the company and/or specific company personnel *and* that is acceptable to top management, as well as to those who will be affected. Also, there are always other items that will need to be added to the questionnaire at this point. Pretest analyses are discussed in greater detail in Chapter 6.

Customer Satisfaction Index

Most companies want an overall satisfaction index that combines and summarizes ratings of all of the attributes. This index can be applied at any or all of several levels: total company, division, sales office, geographic territory, individual service worker, or competitor companies. An example of such an index, which is familiar to nearly everyone, is the J.D. Power Customer Satisfaction Index for automobiles in the United States. There are many ways to construct an index of this type, and these are discussed in Chapter 10. However, it is important to know the purpose of the index and how it will be interpreted and used prior to its development.

Finalize Procedures

When the questionnaire has been constructed and an index model developed, ongoing administration procedures can be finalized. Many procedural questions must be answered, including the following: What groups will be interviewed? How will samples of respondents be selected? What type of survey will be done (e.g., mail, telephone, Internet)? Who will conduct ongoing surveys? How often? Who will analyze ratings and prepare reports? What types of analyses will be done? Who will be the internal custodian of the customer satisfaction program? To whom does this person report? Decisions and plans at this point will produce the track on which the program will run on an ongoing basis.

Types of Satisfaction Rating Scales

Choosing a rating scale that fits a company's customer satisfaction program objectives is extremely important, yet many companies make this choice casually. Some companies are not even aware that they have any options, so they employ simple performance rating scales of the type most often used in conventional market research. Two of the major objectives of this book are to make companies aware that they do have options and to examine each of these options in some detail. This should lead to more appropriate, informed choices when designing CSM programs. There are 4 general types of rating scales that can be used by customers to evaluate the companies that serve them. At this point, we describe each briefly. In Chapters 7 and 8, we examine each of them in greater detail to help companies select the one or ones most suitable for their own objectives.

Simple Performance Rating Scales (Figure 1.8)

Performance rating scales are the easiest to construct and, therefore, are widely used. There are 2 principal types of performance measurement scales: numerical and verbal. The former has verbal statements only at each end to anchor the scale, whereas the latter scale defines *each interval* on the scale. There is no general consensus as to which type is best, and both are popular. Some people are more comfortable using verbal scales because these scales seem to define each level clearly; however, the same word can be interpreted very differently by different people. We address this in greater detail later.

The question of how many intervals the scale should contain (either verbal or numerical) is discussed in Chapter 7. The selection of verbal descriptors for each interval of a verbal scale and for the an-

▼ **FIGURE 1.8 SIMPLE PERFORMANCE RATING SCALES**

Performance Only

A. Numerical scales
Anchor statements only

1   10
Very poor   Very good

B. Verbal scales
Each interval is labeled

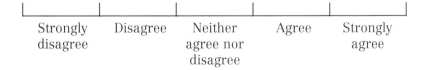

Strongly   Disagree   Neither   Agree   Strongly
disagree   agree nor   agree
                            disagree

chor statements at either end of numerical scales is discussed in both Chapters 2 and 7.

Simple Satisfaction Scale (Figure 1.9)

The simple satisfaction scale is not as widely used as the previous scales, even though it offers a more direct measure of satisfaction. This may be because it does not give a direct measure of either performance or performance in relation to expectations. Both of these are considered useful diagnostics.

Single Expectations/Performance Scale (Figure 1.10)

The single expectations/performance scale provides a way of measuring satisfaction in terms of *meeting customer expectations.* The Baldrige Quality Award uses this criterion, as does the early academic literature on customer satisfaction and dissatisfaction. This approach combines both expectations and performance into a single scale, making the respondent's task easy. One problem is that we do not know whether the customer's original level of expectations is high, medium, or low.

▼ **FIGURE 1.9 SIMPLE SATISFACTION SCALE**

Performance in Relation to Complete Satisfaction

  A. Measurement scale options
    1. Numerical

      1   10
     Not at all   Completely
     satisfied   satisfied

    2. Verbal
        ____ Completely satisfied
        ____ Very satisfied
        ____ Somewhat satisfied
        ____ Not very satisfied
        ____ Not all satisfied

  B. Similar to simple performance ratings

▼ FIGURE 1.10 SINGLE EXPECTATIONS/PERFORMANCE SCALE

Performance in Relation to Expectations

A. Expectations scale

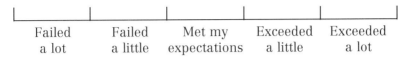

Failed	Failed	Met my	Exceeded	Exceeded
a lot	a little	expectations	a little	a lot

B. Definition of "expectations"
   1. Have a *right* to expect?
   2. Have *come* to expect?

C. Other comparison standards are possible

Another problem is the meaning of the word "expectations." Does it refer to what the customer

• • • has a *right* to expect (performance-based) or
• • • has *come* to expect (experience-based)?

This question is particularly relevant when customers rate products or services they use frequently. In such cases, they know exactly what to expect, based on prior experience (e.g., opening a frequently purchased food or beverage product, going to a McDonald's restaurant). Therefore, it is particularly important to clarify how the respondent is to interpret the word "expectations." The effects of exceeding expectations versus failing expectations on overall satisfaction are discussed in a subsequent chapter.

Instead of expectations, some companies use "best competitor" as the comparison standard. This could mean using the best competitor overall for *all* attributes, or it could mean using the best competitor on *each* attribute separately. (This would have to be made very clear to respondents.) And there are many other possible comparison standards, as discussed in Chapter 8. For now, we focus only on expectations, because this is the original and still the most widely used comparison standard. However, most customer satisfaction programs today probably do *not* use expectations or any other comparison standards in their surveys (see Figure 1.4).

Dual Scaling (Figure 1.11)

The fourth measurement approach can be called *dual scaling*[1] (see Figure 1.9). It requires separate scales (and ratings) for both expectations and performance. This gives us an idea of the absolute level of the respondents' expectations *and* of the performance of a particular product, service, or brand. These scales can be either verbal or numerical, with any number of intervals, but both must be nearly the same. Similar to the single expectations scale, dual scaling defines satisfaction in terms of meeting customer expectations. Therefore, any performance rating below the corresponding expectations rating would be evidence of dissatisfaction. This is called the "expectations–performance gap."

---

[1]The term "dual scaling" also is used for correspondence analysis, a very different technique.

▼ FIGURE 1.11 DUAL SCALING

Separate Scales for Expectations and Performance

A. Expectations

1   10
Very low   Extremely high

B. Performance

1   10
Poor   Excellent

C. Alternatives to expectations
  1. Ideal
  2. Importance ratings
  3. Desired/Wanted
  4. Should be (SERVQUAL)

D. Advantages of dual scaling
  1. Obtain gap scores ("gap analysis") $\Rightarrow$ Unmet needs
  2. Can track expectations over time

Many variations of this scale are possible and, perhaps, desirable. One popular variation is to ask respondents to rate the "importance" of an attribute or feature rather than give their expectations. Then, any performance rating below an importance rating (on the same length of scale) is considered evidence of customer dissatisfaction; some refer to this as the "importance–performance gap." This approach is used widely because it is easily understood and, therefore, has great appeal. However, it also has some drawbacks: First, there is a question as to the semantic equivalence of the words "importance" and "expectations"; most respondents probably would not consider them the same. Second, importance ratings for all attributes often are obtained prior to performance ratings. It would be better psychometric practice to rate importance and performance *at the same time*, in juxtaposition. Third, there is a well-documented tendency for respondents to rate nearly all attributes very high in importance, which makes it difficult to identify the few that really matter. Nevertheless, hard data on some of these points are lacking, so many firms continue to use importance ratings.

Dual scaling has some definite advantages. For one thing, it offers a more precise measure of the *amount* of shortfall or deficiency (as well as surplus) in performance delivery, as compared with the single expectations scale. It also provides some measure of the *absolute level* of prior expectations. Because it does this, it allows tracking of expectations over time, to observe how fast they might be rising and where they might be 3 to 5 years hence. However, dual scaling requires more respondent time, which can result in greater fatigue. There is also some additional cost. In spite of these problems, dual scaling of one kind or another offers many benefits.

Dual scaling for measuring customer satisfaction was popularized in the mid-1980s by Parasuraman, Zeithaml, and Berry (1985). To develop an instrument for measuring *service quality*, they interviewed 4 companies in different service industries (a bank, a credit-card issuer, a repair and maintenance firm, and a long-distance telephone company). After extensive pretesting, they developed an all-purpose measuring instrument called SERVQUAL, which presumably could be used to measure service quality in many service industries. Although this instrument is primarily for service quality, not customer satisfaction, the basic dimensions, many of the rating attributes, and the scaling would be useful for CSM as well. SERVQUAL is discussed in Chapter 8.

All of the preceding scales are discussed in greater detail in subsequent chapters. They are presented here to demonstrate that several options are available to a company starting a CSM program. They also suggest that such programs are more complex than they might seem and that the selection of a measurement scale requires careful thought and analysis for optimum effectiveness.

SUMMARY

The Marketing Concept was a major step forward in formally recognizing the importance of the customer and the marketplace. Many companies benefited greatly from an increased awareness of customers' needs and an internal marketing organization that communicated those needs to other functional areas in the firm. But ultimately, the marketing function failed, in many companies and for many reasons, to make enough of an impact to prevent or ameliorate the 1989–92 economic recession that hurt so many U.S. business firms.

At approximately the same time, the customer satisfaction movement started gathering the momentum it enjoys today. This movement has been much more successful in getting information about customer needs and evaluations directly to the people in the organization who need to act on it, as well as to top management. This chapter describes some of the characteristics of current CSM programs in a sample of 124 large U.S. business firms, including (1) the types of resources used to establish the program, (2) budget allocations, (3) how attributes are chosen, and (4) the type of customer satisfaction model or theory employed.

Four basic types of rating scales are in current use to measure customer satisfaction: (1) simple performance ratings, (2) simple satisfaction scales, (3) single performance/expectations scales, and (4) dual scaling. Each has advantages and limitations, as was discussed briefly in this chapter. All things considered, the approach that provides the most information is usually dual scaling. It also conforms most closely with the original, and still widely used, definition of CSM, and it offers many options in terms of comparison standards.

REFERENCES

Kotler, Philip (1997), *Marketing Management*, 9th ed. Upper Saddle River, NJ: Prentice Hall, 19.

Mentzer, John T., Carol C. Bienstock, and Kenneth B. Kahn (1995), "Benchmarking Satisfaction," *Marketing Management*, 4 (Summer), 41–46.

Naumann, Earl and Kathleen Giel (1995), *Customer Satisfaction Measurement and Management*. Cincinnati, OH: Thomson Executive Press.

Parasuraman, A., Valarie A. Zeithaml, and Leonard Berry (1985), "A Conceptual Model of Service Quality and Its Implications for Future Research," *Journal of Marketing*, 49 (Fall), 41–50.

Webster, Frederick E., Jr. (1997), "The Future Role of Marketing in the Organization," in *Reflections on the Futures of Marketing*, Donald R. Lehmann and Katherine E. Jocz, eds. Cambridge, MA: Marketing Science Institute, 39–66.

CHAPTER 2

DEVELOPING CUSTOMER SATISFACTION SURVEYS

In this chapter, we focus on preliminary planning in the early stages of developing a CSM program for a specific company. Of primary importance is the establishment of program objectives, and several possible objectives are presented and illustrated. It is also important to understand that customer surveys are only one way to obtain useful information, and several other ways are reviewed briefly. Then, sources for obtaining the best assortment of attributes on which the company will be evaluated are discussed. Finally, a brief section on the types of attributes should encourage companies to consider a wide range of topics to be rated.

Focus of the Book

There are many ways to measure customer satisfaction. Some of them are primarily subjective, such as focus groups, one-on-one depth interviews, and the like. Others involve objective measures of one kind or another, for example, number of customer complaints, switching rates, and customer satisfaction surveys. Although all of these can be useful, in this book we focus primarily on

- • • customer satisfaction *surveys* that involve
- • • performance *ratings* on
- • • many *attributes* using
- • • proper rating *scales* plus
- • • *overall* satisfaction measures and
- • • measures of *attribute importance*.

This also would include ratings of such factors as likelihood of switching to another supplier, willingness to recommend present supplier to other companies, and the like. (Some people refer to these as "relationship measures.")

We do not discuss basic survey research techniques such as questionnaire design, question wording, sampling principles and options, or basic analysis. All of these survey topics and more are discussed in any good textbook in marketing research or public opinion polling (see Churchill 1995; Green, Tull, and Albaum 1988). Instead, we emphasize those factors that make CSM different and more complex in some ways than conventional market research surveys. The focus here is primarily on questionnaire design and analysis that is most appropriate for CSM. Accurate and useful CSM is much more difficult than it appears.

POSSIBLE COMPANY OBJECTIVES

The first step in constructing the right CSM program for any company is to *define carefully the objective or objectives*. Because there are so many possible objectives, there cannot be any single best questionnaire design, sample specifications, or analysis plan. Nothing is more important than getting clear guidance from top management about the purposes of the program and how results are to be used and then designing the overall survey to meet these objectives. This can eliminate, or at least greatly reduce, misunderstandings and resistance throughout the firm. Table 2.1 shows several possible objectives or motivations for customer satisfaction programs that have been ob-

▼ TABLE 2.1 POSSIBLE PROGRAM OBJECTIVES AND MOTIVATIONS

- • • Executive curiosity,
- • • Trends over time and comparisons with competition,
- • • Employee compensation,
- • • Key driver analysis to inform the internal allocation of resources,
- • • Internal ownership,
- • • Bottom-line impact, and
- • • Basis for the company mission.

served in a wide variety of companies and industries. We look briefly at each of these.

Executive Curiosity

In the early years of CSM, top management in some companies would commission a single survey to get a quick read on how well the company was satisfying its customers and to see if there were any serious problems. One large health maintenance organization (HMO) did exactly this, asking a sample of its business customers to rate the company on approximately 20 attributes selected by the research department. No attempt was made to determine attribute importance. (At that time, this company was losing approximately 60% of its customers each year! Top management was not concerned, as it believed this could not be helped because price was the only factor operating, and other HMOs also were experiencing high attrition.) Management was satisfied with results from the first survey and did not establish an ongoing measurement program.

Trends and Comparisons

Most companies get beyond simple executive curiosity and feel the need to track customer satisfaction over time, especially for their own companies but also for major competitors. Management then turns to either or both of the following groups: (1) the internal market research department or (2) an outside firm that specializes in customer satisfaction surveys. In many cases, the emphasis is only on establishing a periodic measurement program, without much thought to the internal use or implementation of results.

Employee Compensation

When management believes it must "drive" customer satisfaction into the organization for it to make a difference, management often turns to the "carrot and stick" of employee compensation, generally in the form of additional bonus money. For example, IBM compensates its salespeople on the basis of both sales *profitability* (60%) (not sales volume) and customer satisfaction survey results (40%) (*Business-Week* 1994). At the Electro-Optical Division of Xerox, all employees, from the president down, are affected when compensation decisions are made. The same is true of both a large supplier of industrial products and a large aerospace technology firm, in which executive bonuses can run up to $200,000 to $300,000 per year. This is where the measurement program becomes especially critical!

Key Driver Analysis

It is always important to identify attributes that have the greatest impact and influence on overall satisfaction with the company or any portion thereof. These are the hot buttons discussed in Chapters 3, 4, and 5. Although, as these chapters show, it is extremely difficult to measure them accurately, it is absolutely essential that a serious effort be made to do so. These hot buttons are where company resources must be allocated, because they are the factors that have the greatest impact on overall customer satisfaction and loyalty.

Internal Ownership

When the critical issues and functions have been identified from survey results and analyses, some specific person(s) or group(s) must be held responsible for making the changes that will lead to steady improvement. Some companies call this establishing *ownership* of customer satisfaction survey results. They believe that nothing will change until ownership is clearly established and progress is monitored continuously. Sometimes, a single function within the company is responsible for a certain critical area (e.g., answering the telephone in a prompt and courteous manner); at other times, several disparate functions may be involved (e.g., on-time and accurate delivery).

Bottom-Line Impact

Today's top management wants to know what effect any new company initiative has on the bottom line. This is especially true for internal programs such as TQM, customer satisfaction, and so forth. One retail company CEO said, "It gives me a warm feeling to know that satisfaction is up from 87% to 91%. Now, can someone explain why market share and profitability are down?" A hospital CEO said, "Before I tie my management team's bonus pool to the satisfaction score, I need to be convinced that improving the score is the right thing to do" (Rath & Strong 1997). This type of validation should be designed into a CSM program.

Company Mission

More and more companies are including customer satisfaction in such places as their formal mission statements and/or their annual reports. For example, the 1997 Boeing Annual Report states, "To make the most of (the promising new era), we will concentrate on our three core competencies: detailed customer knowledge and focus; large-scale system integration; and lean, efficient design and production systems. We will listen with care, in order to understand our customers' needs, without pushing our own ideas and technologies." The 1997 Annual Report for Hewlett-Packard states, "The Voice of the Customer. Our job is not just to listen but to hear. We use what customers tell us to understand their current needs more fully as well as to anticipate future needs. That's one way HP can innovate and grow. In 1997, we rededicated ourselves to hearing our customers." And the 1994 Annual Report for AT&T notes, "These past 10 years were neither easy nor without mistakes, however. We were confident at the outset that we knew what customers *needed*. It took time to learn that customer satisfaction is giving customers what they *want*."

Multiple Objectives

Most companies have several of these objectives for their CSM programs. And there is no reason why they should not. Programs of this kind are flexible and can be designed to fulfill a number of objectives concurrently. But these objectives must be clearly specified by management, because any of them can affect the structure, content, and procedures of an ongoing measurement program.

SOURCES OF CUSTOMER SATISFACTION INFORMATION

Before discussing satisfaction surveys in detail, it is important to remember that these surveys are only one way to obtain valuable information about the customer reactions, perceptions, and evaluations that lead to satisfaction with the company's product and/or service offerings. Berry and Parasuraman (1997) propose establishing a complete *information system* to allow ongoing monitoring of all aspects of service quality (a concept related but not identical to customer satisfaction). They suggest research approaches falling into the following 4 major categories:

1. Transactional surveys;
2. Customer complaint, comment, and inquiry capture;
3. Total market surveys; and
4. Employee surveys.

Table 2.2 provides, for each of these categories, their description, purpose, approximate frequency, and some limitations. Information of this kind can serve as a reminder that there are many approaches to measuring satisfaction, in addition to the customer surveys discussed in this book. It would seem that all of these approaches could be profitably adapted for CSM.

▶ TABLE 2.2 RESEARCH APPROACHES FOR BUILDING SERVICE QUALITY INFORMATION SYSTEMS

Type	Description	Purpose	Frequency[†]	Limitations
Transaction-al surveys*	Service satisfaction survey of customers following a service encounter.	Obtain customer feedback while service experience is still fresh; act on feedback quickly if negative patterns develop.	Continuous	Focuses on customers' most recent experience rather than their overall assessment. Noncustomers are excluded.
Mystery shopping	Researchers become "customers" to experience and evaluate the quality of service delivered.	Measure individual employee service behaviors for use in coaching, training, performance evaluation, recognition, and rewards; identify systematic strengths and weaknesses in customer-contact service.	Quarterly	Subjective evaluations; researchers may be more "judgmental" than customers would be; expense limits repetitions; potential to hurt employee morale if improperly used.
New-, declining-, and lost-customer surveys	Surveys to determine why customers select the firm, reduce their buying, or leave the firm.	Assess the role service quality and other issues play in customer patronage and loyalty.	Continuous	Firm must be able to identify and monitor service usage on a per-customer basis.

TABLE 2.2 CONTINUED

Type	Description	Purpose	Frequency†	Limitations
Focus group interviews	Directed questioning of a small group, usually 8 to 12 people. Questions focus on a specific topic. Can be used with customer, noncustomer, or employee groups.	Provide a forum for participants to suggest service improvement ideas; offer fast, informal feedback on service issues.	As needed	Dynamics of group interview may prevent certain issues from surfacing. Focus groups are, in effect, brainstorming sessions; the information generated is not projectable to the population of interest. Focus group research is most valuable when coupled with projectable research.
Customer advisory panels	A group of customers recruited to periodically provide the firm with feedback and advice on service performance and other issues. Data are obtained in meetings, over the telephone, through mail questionnaires, or by other means. Employee panels also can be formed.	Obtain in-depth, timely feedback and suggestions about service quality from experienced customers who cooperate because of "membership" nature of the panel.	Quarterly	May not be projectable to entire customer base. Excludes noncustomers. Panelists may assume role of "expert" and become less representative of customer base.

TABLE 2.2 CONTINUED

Type	Description	Purpose	Frequency†	Limitations
Service reviews	Periodic visits with customers (or a class of customers) to discuss and assess the service relationship. Should be a formal process with a common set of questions, capture of responses in a database, and follow-up communication with customers.	Identify customer expectations and perceptions of the company's service performance and improvement priorities in a face-to-face conversation. A view of the future, not just a study of the past. Opportunity to include multiple decision makers and decision influencers in the discussions.	Annually or semiannually	Time consuming and expensive. Most appropriate for firms marketing complex services on an ongoing, relationship basis.
Customer complaint, comment, and inquiry capture*	System to retain, categorize, track, and distribute customer complaints and other communications with the company.	Identify most common types of service failure for corrective action. Identify, through customer communications, opportunities to improve service or otherwise strengthen customer relationships.	Continuous	Dissatisfied customers frequently do not complain directly to the company. Analysis of customer complaints and comments offers only a partial picture of the state of service.

TABLE 2.2 CONTINUED

Type	Description	Purpose	Frequency[+]	Limitations
Total market surveys	Surveys that measure customers' overall assessment of a company's service. Research includes both external customers and competitors' customers, that is, the total market.	Assess company's service performance compared with competitors; identify service improvement priorities; track service improvement over time.	Semiannually or quarterly	Measures customers' overall service assessments but does not capture assessments of specific service encounters.
Employee field reporting	Formal process for gathering, categorizing, and distributing field employee intelligence about service issues.	Capture and share at the management level intelligence about customers' service expectations and perceptions gathered in the field.	Continuous to monthly	Some employees will be more conscientious and efficient reporters than others. Employees may be unwilling to provide negative information to management.

TABLE 2.2 CONTINUED

Type	Description	Purpose	Frequency[†]	Limitations
Employee surveys	Surveys regarding the service employees provide and receive and the quality of their work lives.	Measure internal service quality; identify employee-perceived obstacles to improved service; track employee morale and attitudes. Employee surveys help answer "why" service performance is what it is.	Quarterly	The strength of employee surveys is also a weakness; employees view service delivery from their own vantage point, subject to their own biases. Employees can offer valuable insights into the root causes of service problems but are not always objective or correct in their interpretations.
Service operating data capture	A system to retain, categorize, track, and distribute key service performance operating data, such as service response times, failure rates, and delivery costs.	Monitor service performance indicators and take corrective action to improve performance as necessary. Relate operating performance data to customer and employee feedback.	Continuous	Operating performance data may not be relevant to customers' perceptions of service. Focus is on what is occurring but not why.

*Highlighted approach normally would be part of *any* service quality information system.
†Frequencies of use vary among companies.
Source: Berry, Leonard L. and A. Parasuraman (1997), "Listening to the Customer—The Concept of a Service-Quality Information System," *Sloan Management Review*, 38 (Spring), 65–76. © 1997, Sloan Management Review. All rights reserved.

SELECTING SURVEY ATTRIBUTES

The heart of a customer satisfaction survey is usually ratings of *performance* on several selected attributes plus measures of *overall satisfaction*, *loyalty*, and *switching intentions*. To implement such a survey, some companies follow a simplistic recipe: Select some product and/or service attributes the company believes customers think are most important, select an appropriate rating scale (any kind of scale will do), and conduct the survey using the mail or telephone. There is no more to it than that. Some larger companies call in research firms that specialize in customer satisfaction surveys, and this is sometimes recommended. But many medium-sized or smaller companies (and even some larger ones) proceed on their own or contract with smaller marketing research firms that have little or no experience in customer satisfaction research. These are the companies that will probably benefit most from this book.

As an aside, hiring a research firm that specializes in CSM is not always the best approach, even for large firms that can afford the best services. Some specialty firms use a "cookie-cutter" approach and try to fit every problem into their own standardized approach instead of working with the client to determine exactly what is needed for a particular situation or objective. In such cases, large client firms will find that books such as this can help present options and alternatives to consider before designing their own system or when deciding among competing outside specialty research firms.

Arguably, the single most important component of a customer satisfaction survey is the set of attributes respondents are asked to rate. Most companies believe that the real value of a survey is knowing precisely where the company is delivering satisfactorily and, especially, where it is failing to live up to customers' expectations or desires. In this sense, results from these surveys can determine the allocation of major company efforts and resources to improve satisfaction among customers. This means that the proper selection of attributes to be rated is of utmost importance. Anything that is not included in the questionnaire *from the beginning* cannot be recovered later during the analysis!

Although it is always wise to survey employees in key positions informally to get their suggestions as to what company attributes should be rated by customers, their responses should be considered with caution. Even though knowledgeable people understand (or believe they understand) what is important to customers, they might not know exactly how to state or phrase an attribute to get at the core of an issue—the hot button. An example will help illustrate.

In a customer satisfaction study involving clients of an industrial products company, management decided to include several attributes relating to the ongoing service provided by its salespeople. These included the following:

• • • Representative is always available.
• • • Attention is paid to our account.
• • • Representative understands our needs.
• • • Representative knows his or her own product line.
• • • Representative is responsive to specific problems.

Although all of these were found to be important in driving overall satisfaction with the supplier, "responsive to specific problems" was more important than the others by a clear margin. Yet, it had not been included in the original set of attributes selected by management. (It was added later on a trial basis by the research firm that conducted the interviews.) Getting just the right wording or perspective for an issue is critical, but it can be very difficult.

Focus Groups

Many firms believe that the single best source of attributes is focus group interviews conducted with a small sample of customers, former customers, competitors' customers, and/or prospective customers. Often, these groups are selected to be homogeneous in terms of one or more demographic characteristics (for consumers) or industry types or sizes (for business firms), though satisfaction survey objectives will dictate the composition of each group. Competent, experienced moderators are a must, but competence can vary widely. It is wise to prescreen moderators by asking to attend sessions conducted by them for other clients or, at least, to review some videotapes involving different moderators, when possible.

However, the feasibility of focus groups varies widely from one company situation to another. Focus groups are most useful when customers or clients are concentrated in a few geographic areas (usually larger cities) so that participants can be assembled easily and at low cost. They are least feasible when customers are scattered widely across the United States or even the world, as they often are in business-to-business marketing. In such cases, some companies conduct their focus groups by telephone conference calls or videoconferencing (e.g., Focus Vision Inc.). Sometimes companies can take advantage of forthcoming trade shows or conferences by assembling groups from the attendees.

Depth Interviews

Some product and/or service categories have users that are hard to assemble into a single location (e.g., doctors, senior management, design engineers). Or, the category might comprise products and/or services that are personal or sensitive in one way or another (e.g., personal care products, financial or health services). Companies in these businesses sometimes elect to conduct one-on-one depth interviews with users or potential users. This makes it easier for trained interviewers to get beneath the surface and probe people's innermost feelings and problems, and some very useful attributes can emerge.

It is also very helpful to conduct interviews with the champion(s) of the customer satisfaction program within the company. This can yield important insights into the purpose and objectives of the program, as well as into how the findings are to be used. In turn, these insights can dictate such factors as the topic areas to be covered in the survey, as well as the specific attributes to be rated by customers and other types of respondents.

Former Customers

One source that often is overlooked is people or firms that have decided *not to rebuy or resubscribe*. Some of these former customers have valid reasons for defecting that have nothing to do with price or satisfaction with a product or service (e.g., moved away, gone out of business, acquired by another business firm). But others are deeply dissatisfied with the product or service itself or with after-sale service. One study found that approximately 40% of former customers had left because of poor service of one kind or another, not to get a lower price. Depth interviews with these people should uncover the factors that have the greatest effect on loyalty, as well as on satisfaction.

Previous Research

Most companies of any size conduct market research on an ongoing basis. Although the objectives of these studies may vary widely, some contain findings that are appropriate and useful for customer satisfaction surveys. It never hurts to review the contents and findings of prior research to pick up comments and complaints that could suggest attributes to be rated by customers. Some of the same issues might appear over and over in various studies, and the different results can suggest better ways of phrasing statements to be rated.

All Important Attributes?

How does a company know that all the attributes that are most important to customers have been identified? Even with a surfeit of ideas or statements, there is never any guarantee that all important issues have been included in the final list. Both management and research personnel tend toward logical, rational, and functional criteria in the selection of statements to be rated. Statements that reflect affective factors and feelings are often overlooked, for example, "Treats me like a valued customer" or "Makes me feel important." Yet these might be (and sometimes are) more important to customers than specific functional performance attributes.

Even though there is no sure way of knowing a priori on a judgmental basis if all important ideas are included in a final survey format, this can be estimated statistically. One useful approach is to perform a multiple regression of the performance ratings on all attributes in the pretest versus some measure of overall satisfaction with the company. This measure could include, for example,

• • • overall satisfaction rating, all things considered;
• • • actual repurchase frequency;
• • • likelihood of switching suppliers/brands;
• • • willingness to recommend company;

or some combination of these. Many companies use a weighted composite of several, or even all, of these as a single *loyalty index measure*, which can serve as the dependent variable in a regression analysis (see Chapter 11). If the multiple R^2 is, say, 70%–80% or better, there is good reason to believe that most of the really important ideas have been included.[1] If it is 50% or less, this strongly suggests that some important ideas have been omitted. This is another reason why a pretest is always strongly recommended.

TYPES OF ATTRIBUTES

Another perspective when deciding which attributes to include is to consider the different *types of attributes* that might be relevant. One attempt to provide a taxonomy of attributes is shown next. It proposes that there are 5 major types of product/service attributes, all of

---

[1]R^2 is the percentage of the variation in the overall satisfaction measure(s) that is explained or accounted for by all of the rated attributes combined.

which should be considered in developing any customer satisfaction or market research survey (Myers 1996, pp. 298–99):

• • • physical product characteristics/features,
• • • benefits wanted,
• • • personal imagery,
• • • company imagery, and
• • • ultimate personal goals/values.

Examples of each of these appear in Figure 2.1 for attributes that were used in a survey for women's hair shampoos. Of course, these types will have differential importance for different product and/or service categories. For example, company imagery attributes have been found to be especially relevant for products and/or services for which the buyer has some degree of uncertainty and/or lacks knowledge. Examples include health care services, pet foods, insurance, children's toys, organic foods, and mainframe computers. In these cases, many buyers look more carefully at the company behind the product. They want a company they can trust, one that has been around for a long time, or the one that has the biggest market share. In contrast, physical product characteristics or features that people can evaluate for themselves are usually more important for food and beverage products.

This does not mean that all 5 types of attributes must be included in every customer satisfaction survey. It only suggests that each type should be considered carefully (and preferably tested) in terms of the objectives of the survey, the nature of the product and/or service, and the characteristics of customers. For example, it is easy to overlook a subjective attribute such as "Treats me like a valued customer," though it has often been found to be of great importance (and sometimes the greatest importance) in satisfaction surveys.

The attributes in Figure 2.1 are especially useful to keep in mind when developing a long list of attributes for a pretest. Then, careful analysis of pretest results can show which general types of attributes are most important for customer satisfaction with a particular product and/or service category and can point to specific items within these general types that are best for the final set of perhaps 15 to 25 attributes to be rated on an ongoing basis. It is important to remember to include attributes that refer to *specific internal functional areas* that serve customers in one way or another, so that evaluations can be traced back for corrective action as needed.

1. Physical Characteristics/Features

- Contains protein
- Has lots of lather
- Has pH balance
- Has a light color
- Is concentrated
- Has a strong aroma

2. Benefits Wanted

- Cleans the hair
- Leaves hair manageable
- Is gentle
- Rinses out easily
- Doesn't irritate scalp
- Has a nice fragrance

3. Personal Imagery

- Leaves hair young-looking
- Gives hair a sexy look
- Is recommended by hairdressers
- Used by friends
- Is old-fashioned
- Gives user a glamorous look

4. Company Imagery

- Made by a company user can trust
- Company has a long history
- Company's products are superior
- Company has developed a lot of good new shampoo products
- Company is a leader in hair care technology/preparation

5. Ultimate Personal Goals/Values

- Always helps users look their very best
- User feels very confident about hair after using this shampoo
- Using this shampoo gives user peace of mind
- User's hair looks so good people notice it

THE ATTRIBUTE LIFE CYCLE

In his book *Managing Customer Value*, Gale (1994) proposes the interesting idea that product and/or service attributes can have life cycles of their own. When he facilitates what he calls a "quality profiling session" with management in his client firms, he often asks participants to place each attribute they are considering into 1 of the 7 stages that make up his attribute life cycle (Figure 2.2), as follows:

▼ FIGURE 2.2 STAGES OF THE ATTRIBUTE LIFE CYCLE

1 Latent: Not yet visible or apparent.

2 Desired: Known but not currently supplied—no weight.

----

3 Unique: Only the pioneer scores well—some weight.

4 Pacing: One supplier is already ahead and weight is shifting onto this attribute.

5 Key: Differences in performance determine competitiveness:
            Niche attribute—important in one segment.
            Power attribute—important in all segments.

6 Fading: Catch-up moves and/or declining weight begin to take away the top performer's competitive edge.

----

7 Basic: All suppliers perform well—no competitive edge; required, expected; no weight unless performance declines.

Source: Gale, Bradley T. (1994), *Managing Customer Value: Creating Quality and Service that Customers Can See*. New York: The Free Press. © 1994, Bradley T. Gale.

1. A *latent* attribute is not visible or apparent. These attributes lie hidden in the minds of customers and designers. Companies use probing questions and float ideas to customers in an attempt to uncover what customers desire.
2. A *desired* attribute is known but not currently supplied by any competitor. It will become a unique attribute when some supplier fulfills the need. As people experience the benefits of this attribute without fully anticipating them, it will provide unexpected quality.
3. For a *unique* attribute, only one supplier, the pioneer, scores well. Therefore, the pioneer commands a big advantage with the customer segment that weights this attribute heavily. If the benefits of this attribute are unexpected or only partially expected, customers, as they buy or switch to this product supplier for the first time, will react with delight.
4. An attribute is in the *pacing* stage when one supplier is ahead and weight is shifting to this attribute. If it attracts enough weight, it will become a key attribute.
5. Differences in performance on *key* attributes determine competitiveness. An attribute that is key to only one segment is a *niche* attribute. A key attribute that is important in all segments of the targeted market is a *power* attribute.
6. As catch-up moves and/or declining weight take away the top performer's competitive edge, a key attribute becomes a *fading* attribute.
7. An attribute reaches the *basic* stage when all suppliers in the buyers' consideration set perform well. No supplier has a competitive

edge. The attribute is required and typically receives little weight in the supplier selection decision. But buyers will react to a decline in performance on these attributes and remove that supplier's business from consideration.

When a supplier pulls ahead of the pack on an emerging attribute at the beginning of the life cycle, customers tend to react very positively. When an attribute is in stages 3 through 5, buyers make a more deliberate assessment of performance. When a supplier slips in performance on a basic attribute, buyers tend to react negatively.

To stay at the cutting edge of quality leadership, a company needs to innovate continuously or achieve top performance on key attributes. Seventy-year-old Gillette, the quality and category leader in male grooming products, derives 35 percent of its sales from products it has introduced in the past five years (Gale 1994, p. 135).

Customer Satisfaction Surveys

What type or types of attributes should be used in customer satisfaction surveys? Probably the best place to start would be with key attributes, because these are, by definition, the ones Gale believes "determine competitiveness." These would be critical for at least one segment of customers and perhaps for all customers. Key attributes are the ones companies must deliver on if they are to retain their present customers and maintain market share. They are also important in attracting and holding new customers.

It is probably wise to include some fading and even basic attributes in customer surveys as well. These may not have the impact that key attributes have, but they are still required. Even though a company receives no special credit for them, because all major competitors offer them also, customers will be offended if key attributes are absent or weak. A company could also include 1 or 2 unique or pacing attributes, especially if it excels on them.

REFERENCES

Berry, Leonard L. and A. Parasuraman (1997), "Listening to the Customer—The Concept of a Service-Quality Information System," *Sloan Management Review*, 38 (Spring), 65–76.

BusinessWeek (1994), "IBM Leans On Its Sales Force," (February 7), 110.

Churchill, Gilbert A. (1995), *Marketing Research: Methodological Foundations*, 6th ed. Hinsdale, IL: The Dryden Press.

Gale, Bradley T. (1994), *Managing Customer Value: Creating Quality and Service that Customers Can See*. New York: The Free Press.

Green, Paul E., Donald S. Tull, and Gerald Albaum (1988), *Research for Marketing Decisions*, 5th ed. Englewood Cliffs, NJ: Prentice Hall.

Myers, James H. (1996), *Segmentation and Positioning for Strategic Marketing Decisions*. Chicago: American Marketing Association.

Rath & Strong, Management Consultants (1997), presentation at Institute for International Research, Conference on Market Segmentation, New York (October).

CHAPTER 3

DIRECT METHODS OF MEASURING ATTRIBUTE IMPORTANCE

I n this and the following 2 chapters, we discuss several different ways to determine the *relative importance of the company attributes* used to measure customer satisfaction. Some of these methods ask respondents outright to indicate their beliefs about the importance of each attribute, usually with some kind of measurement scale or format. These direct methods are discussed in this chapter. The following 2 chapters show several ways of deriving or inferring attribute importance from responses to indirect rating tasks or formats. Respondents are not asked to give their own evaluations of importance and often are unaware that this is even an objective.

The search for attributes to be rated in customer satisfaction surveys usually yields a large number of possibilities. Many of these attributes are relatively unimportant or overlap other similar attributes that are very important, so they do not need to be included in a final measuring instrument. Others are of key importance in driving such critical factors as overall satisfaction, loyalty, switching intentions, and the value of a customer to the bottom line. Therefore, companies need some way or ways of identifying these "hot buttons" to help them decide which attributes need to be measured in their on-going customer satisfaction surveys and where to focus their follow-up improvement efforts.

Measuring attribute importance has been a continuously vexing problem for companies in all types of businesses. It has led to a pro-liferation of measurement methods and approaches that can be used within the format of typical market research or customer satisfaction surveys. Some of these approaches are quite simple and have great in-tuitive appeal. Others can be obscure and extremely complex in both design and analysis. Unfortunately, different approaches often pro-duce different results, sometimes very different (Griffin and Hauser 1993; Heeler, Okechuku, and Reid 1979; Jaccard, Brinberg, and Ack-erman 1986). Were it not for the obvious necessity of the task, this problem alone would discourage many business firms from even at-tempting to determine the importance of product and/or service at-tributes. And indeed, some companies make very little effort to do so.

Knowing the relative importance of attributes can be useful for de-veloping a satisfaction measurement program in at least three ways:

1. In a *pretest*, it enables us to eliminate some attributes that have lit-tle or no impact on satisfaction, thereby reducing to a minimum the number of items included in the final, ongoing tracking surveys.
2. In the *final survey*, it enables us to weight the attribute ratings on the basis of their importance when constructing a customer satis-faction index.
3. In an *ongoing program*, it provides a guide for management to fo-cus company resources on improving functions that have the great-est impact on satisfying customers. These are the hot buttons com-panies must work on the most.

Because of the importance of this matter, and because different approaches yield different results, we would expect that most compa-nies would make an extra effort to measure the importance of the at-tributes in their customer satisfaction surveys in several different ways. This usually is not the case.

DIRECT VERSUS INDIRECT METHODS

Although many scholars and practitioners have addressed the problem of how to measure the relative importance of the attributes of an object or person, a cohesive framework for all these efforts does not seem to exist. Specific techniques have been developed ad hoc to fit a wide variety of needs and objectives, but few attempts have been made to relate these to one another or even to compare results from different approaches for the same topic area and attributes. In the absence of a formal conceptual framework, we suggest a simple one: direct versus indirect methods. Most specific approaches can be fitted rather clearly into one or the other of these categories.

Briefly, direct methods consist of those that are "transparent" to the respondent. Respondents understand that they are being asked to indicate how important a given attribute or product feature is to them, using any one of several formats. In these formats, direct methods usually involve only a simple task for the respondent, and results are easily understood and interpreted by client management. Unfortunately, many of these methods have some major problems and weaknesses, as we discuss next. Still, they are popular because they are relatively straightforward and have great intuitive appeal.

In contrast, indirect methods tend to be rather obscure to respondents. For most of these methods, it is not likely that most respondents know they are being asked to indicate how important a given attribute or feature is (though there is no real evidence on this point). None of the instructions to the respondent indicates or even suggests what the outcome will be or how the results will be used. Indirect methods often involve more complicated tasks for respondents than direct measures do, and from respondent ratings of one sort or another, the importance of attributes is *inferred* or *derived* on the basis of a statistical analysis of the data. Therefore, these methods are less likely to have intuitive appeal, and many persons in management are not completely comfortable with results based on indirect methods. The following methods, both direct and indirect, are described and discussed here.

Direct methods:

- • • elicitation,
- • • importance ratings,
- • • constant sum,
- • • paired comparisons,
- • • determinance, and
- • • laddering (means-end chain).

Indirect methods:

- • • correlation/regression,
- • • conjoint analysis (full profile),
- • • conjoint analysis (pairwise trade-offs),
- • • extreme differences,
- • • indifference level,
- • • computerized semiotics, and
- • • strategic cube analysis.

In this chapter, we review several direct methods that are likely to be the most useful for both researchers and management. Most are simple to understand and execute, even though the required analytics are not simple for some. For each method, we provide a few of the more obvious advantages and limitations, though we make no claim that these are exhaustive. Each method's strengths and weaknesses clearly imply that there is no single "best" approach. Each user must select the method that is most appropriate for the circumstances, budget, preferences of management and other users, and his or her own convictions. However, some comparisons of results from several of these methods are presented in Chapter 6 to help select an appropriate one or ones for a specific application. Some overall recommendations also are made.

DIRECT METHODS

Elicitation

Probably the simplest of all approaches to measuring attribute importance is the one often referred to as "elicitation" (see Griffin and Hauser 1993; Jaccard, Brinberg, and Ackerman 1986). It is based on the proposition that if you want to know what is important to people, you should just ask them. Questions to respondents might be, "What are the most important features you want in a (boat, shampoo, automobile, and such)?" or, "What are the most important features you look for when buying a ...?" Advantages and limitations include, but are not limited to, the following:

Advantages

- • • It is easy for respondent to understand and express;
- • • It has intuitive appeal for management and other users; and
- • • It is easy to execute, analytics are simple (e.g., tallies of responses).

Disadvantages

- • • It might exceed ability of respondent to answer,
- • • It might exceed willingness of respondent to answer,
- • • Usually only a few attributes are given by each respondent,
- • • It oversimplifies complex products and/or services, and
- • • It often merely reflects advertising claims.

The first two disadvantages are well known to experienced survey professionals and are explained in most textbooks in marketing research and public opinion polling. Sometimes people do not really understand what influences them the most, or they temporarily forget important aspects of a product or service. When reporting satisfaction, customers might overreport one or two irritating problem areas and fail to mention other aspects that are quite satisfactory or even superior. Sometimes respondents know what is most important to them but are unwilling to express this for fear of appearing subjective or irrational (e.g., styling or color, influence of advertising, peer or family pressure, like or dislike of salesperson). People usually try to appear sensible and rational.

Also, because respondents tend to name only a few attributes, elicitation is particularly inappropriate for products and/or services that are complex for the user. Examples of these would include casual dining restaurants, consumer photography, automobiles, and some types of financial services. In addition, many people simply mention advertising copy claims ("they tell us what we have told them"). Most research professionals believe that elicitation results are usually dubious and of limited utility.

Importance Ratings

Another simple method with intuitive appeal involves importance ratings. Respondents are asked to rate the importance of several selected product and/or service attributes, usually on a 7- or 10-point scale. For example,

Please rate the importance to you of each of the following attributes of a personal computer (PC):

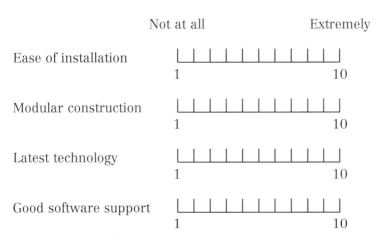

Of course, any other type or length of scale could be used as well, as discussed in Chapter 7.

Advantages

• • • It is easy for respondents to understand;
• • • It provides interval-scale measures (or quasi-interval), which are helpful in later analyses; and
• • • It is credible to upper management, makes sense.

Disadvantages

• • • It might exceed ability of respondent to answer,
• • • It might exceed willingness of respondent to answer,
• • • It has too many top-box ratings, and
• • • Researcher might omit some very important attributes.

Table 3.1 is particularly instructive in demonstrating the problem of too many top-box ratings. It came from a proprietary survey of 1000 customers of a large utility company in the United States. Note that 15 of the 30 attributes (half) had mean (average) importance ratings between approximately 9.6 and 9.8 on a 10-point scale! Only 5 attributes had mean scores below 9.0. Findings of this kind have appeared in many other studies conducted by this writer, as well as by others. They offer little guidance in informing management decisions and planning activities.

There is also the very real possibility that we might inadvertently omit one or more important attributes from those to be rated by respondents. (One way around the problem of too many high ratings, which has been used successfully by some analysts, is to either center or standardize ratings for each respondent separately [intraindividual]. In this way, every respondent has a mean rating of 0 over all attributes rated, and the relative importance of attributes is measured in relation to this.[1])

In spite of their great intuitive appeal and frequent usage, importance ratings should be used with caution and preferably in combination with other methods, especially indirect ones, for identifying hot buttons. An example of how this might be achieved is shown in the "Cost of Entry" section at the end of Chapter 5.

---

[1]Comment by Gary Mullet, Gary Mullet Inc.

▼ TABLE 3.1 RATED IMPORTANCE OF UTILITY COMPANY PROGRAMS AND ACTIVITIES

Activities	Mean Importance Rating*
Top importance activities	
Effectively handles emergencies	9.79
Maintains reliable source of energy	9.76
Does the job right the first time	9.74
Restores service quickly	9.72
Accurate meter reading and billing	9.69
Competent and well-trained employees	9.69
Resolves problems quickly	9.68
Relatively stable rates	9.66
Tries to keep rates low	9.66
Provides consistent energy	9.65
Provides safety information	9.63
Plans effectively for the future	9.60
Takes steps to not harm the environment	9.60
Cost-conscious	9.59
Provides safety checks	9.59
Middle-range importance activities	
Makes service calls at convenient hours	9.48
Treats customers as if valued	9.42
Programs to help seniors and low-income customers	9.29
Convenient hours to call	9.28
Polite and courteous employees	9.26
Offers programs to help control costs	9.20
Provides appliance adjustments and relights	9.20
Keeps customers well-informed	9.06
Answers phone promptly	9.06
Efficient in number of employees	9.04
Lower-range importance activities	
Offers optional rate plans	8.91
Involved with local community	8.80
Convenient office hours	8.37
Convenient office locations	8.10
Contributes money to worthy causes	7.96

*10-point scale.

Instead of ratings, some companies prefer to ask respondents to *rank order* the importance of attributes. In a recent customer satisfaction survey for a manufacturer of oil drilling equipment, respondents were asked to rank the importance of 15 attributes for 5 different applications of this equipment, for a total of 75 ranks. However, this places a greater burden on respondents because ranks are much more difficult to assign than are ratings (the top and bottom 3 or 4 ranks are not nearly as hard as the ones in between). Also, this gives firms no information about the psychological distance between ranks. For example, the attribute with a rank of 1 might be much more important than the one with a rank of 2, or it might be only slightly more important. Ranking is probably not as good as rating, especially for applications with more than 5 to 10 attributes.

Constant Sum

One prior attempt to surmount the problem of too many high ratings is known as the "constant sum" method (Aaker, Kumar, and Day 1998, pp. 281–82). The respondent is asked to allocate a fixed number of points (usually 10 or 100) over several product and/or service attributes in terms of their relative importance. For example, a questionnaire might ask the following:

Please consider a situation in which you might be purchasing a microcomputer for your own business (or for home use). For each situation, please allocate 100 points among the services listed according to their *relative importance* to you. For example, if proper installation and immediate troubleshooting help are the only two services that are important to you, allocate the entire 100 points *between* them. And if troubleshooting is twice as important as installation, it should be allocated approximately twice as many points:

Installation	35
Troubleshooting	65
Fits in a small space	0
Can play video games	0
	100 points

Advantages

• • • It forces trade-offs,
• • • It prevents checking top box for nearly all attributes, and
• • • Analysis is simple.

Disadvantages

- • • It is best when only small numbers of attributes are presented (≤ 10);
- • • It is an "ipsative" (relative) scale, no anchors or reference points;
- • • Respondent might not be able to add to 100 (careless errors); and
- • • Researcher might omit some important attributes.

This method makes it much more difficult for respondents to assign high ratings to nearly all the attributes. As a result, it forces a trade-off of the importance of one attribute against others. Faced with this requirement, respondents seldom give the same number of points to all attributes. They are reluctant to "use up" points on attributes that are less important than others. It is assumed that this forces them to sharpen their thinking.

When the number of attributes is large, as it would tend to be for complex products and/or services, respondents may not believe they have enough points to enable them to highlight several really important factors. The number of points can always be increased, but this also increases complexity for the respondent. In addition, there is the possibility of careless errors when allocating points that do not add to 10, 100, 200, or so forth, especially for larger numbers of points. Therefore, this method is most useful when the number of attributes is rather small.

Although the constant sum method can be very useful in some situations, it has significant limitations for others. A major conceptual problem is the ipsative scale, with no reference points, that this method uses. All attributes might be of high importance, or of medium or low importance, and this would not be known. Therefore, for several reasons, the constant sum method is not nearly as widely used as some of the other direct methods.

Paired Comparisons

Another direct method that is especially simple for respondents is known as "paired comparisons" (see Green and Tull 1978). Respondents are presented with *all possible pairs of attributes*, one pair at a time. They are asked to indicate which of the two attributes is most important to them. An actual example from a recent study of laptop PC screens is shown in Table 3.2. Only a few of the 55 possible pairs of eleven attributes are shown.

Table 3.3 shows how importance scale values are calculated on the basis of the proportions of respondents who say that the column attribute is more important than the row attribute. Those proportions

For each pair of attributes, please check the one that is most important to you.

No color change with viewing angle	☐	or	Higher resolution	☐
Lower cost	☐	or	Wider viewing angle	☐
Higher resolution	☐	or	Higher contrast	☐
Wider viewing angle	☐	or	Better color fidelity	☐
Higher contrast	☐	or	Better sunlight viewability	☐
Better color fidelity	☐	or	More CRT-like pixels	☐

▼ TABLE 3.3 PAIRED COMPARISONS ANALYSIS

	A	B	C	D	E
A. No damage	(.50)	.82	.69	.25	.35
B. Cleans hair	.18	(.50)	.27	.07	.15
C. Manageable	.31	.73	(.50)	.16	.25
D. Amt. aroma	.75	.93	.84	(.50)	.59
E. Convenient	.65	.85	.75	.41	(.50)
Scale values:	−.09	+1.21	+.43	−.57	−.92
(Rescaled):	(.83)	(2.13)	(1.35)	(.35)	(.00)

Notes: Table entries are proportions of respondents saying column attribute is more important than row attribute. From Green, Paul E. and Donald Tull (1978), *Research for Marketing Decisions*. Englewood Cliffs, NJ: Prentice Hall, p. 183.

are shown as table entries. The proportions must first be transformed into "z" scale values and then added down each column to get importance scale values (using Thurstone Case V scaling). These values can then be rescaled to remove the negatives by adding the lowest scale value (.92) to each sum. In this way, simple paired comparisons judgments can produce *scale values of relative importance* for a total sample of respondents or for any subsample.

Advantages

• • • It transforms simple paired comparisons (i.e., rank ordered judgments) into scale values that reflect the relative importance of each attribute or feature;

• • • It forces trade-offs, respondents can't check both; and

• • • It is an easy task for respondents.

Disadvantages

• • • It is feasible for only a few attributes;

• • • Scale values can be determined only at the aggregate level, not for each respondent;

• • • It produces ipsative scale values; and

• • • Analysis is more difficult than it is for preceding direct methods.

Perhaps the biggest problem is the large number of comparisons that must be made when the number of attributes is large. Even though most comparisons are rather easy for respondents, the sheer number of them can be a burden. The task gets especially onerous when there are more than 10 to 15 attributes. For example, 10 attributes require 45 paired comparisons, 15 require 105. Usually, larger numbers simply would not be feasible. Also, importance scale values are meaningful and precise only for a *sample* of respondents, not for a single respondent, in contrast to the 3 methods discussed previously. However, paired comparisons can be very useful when the number of attributes is small, and it probably yields more accurate results than any of the preceding direct methods.

One way to get around the problem of a large number of pairs is to ask each respondent to rate only a subsample of these pairs, making sure that each pair is evaluated approximately the same number of times overall. Of course, this requires a larger sample of respondents.[2]

Determinance

The idea behind the determinance concept is that an attribute can be very important and yet not matter much to a customer in evaluating a company or supplier (see Alpert 1971; Myers and Alpert 1968). For example, it is very important that our cars start right away in the morning, that our money is safe in a bank, and that our airliner doesn't fall out of the sky. But do these things really matter? Not if all cars start right up and all major banks and airlines are considered equally safe. Some years ago, Nelson Foote (1961, p. 11) of General Electric put it this way:

> In the electrical appliance business, we have been impressed over and over
> by the way in which certain characteristics of products come to be taken for

---

[2]Comment by Gary Mullet, Gary Mullet Inc.

granted by consumers, especially those concerned with basic functional performance, or with values like safety. If these values are missing in a product, the user is extremely offended. But if they are present, the maker or seller gets no special credit or preference, because quite logically every other maker and seller is assumed to be offering equivalent values.

In other words, the values that are salient in decision making are the values that are problematic—that are important, to be sure, but also those which differentiate one offering from another.

What this suggests is that, in addition to measuring the importance of an attribute, we need to measure the extent to which it is *perceived to vary* among competing entries in the marketplace. This can be done by asking respondents to rate both the importance of an attribute and the perceived *amount of difference* of this attribute among the major competitors in a product and/or service category. Attributes that are offered approximately equally by all suppliers cannot be expected to have a great influence on overall customer satisfaction (unless they are missing). The following is an example from a study of writing instruments:

Respondents were asked to rate ballpoint and fountain pens on 11 attributes (e.g., firm grip, appearance, doesn't skip), using the following questions: (1) How *important* is each of these attributes in your own choice of a pen? and (2) How much *difference* do you believe there is among these brands in each of these attributes?

Determinance scores for each attribute in this study were derived by multiplying the importance and difference rated values on a 5-point interval scale.

Advantages

• • • It identifies attributes that are important to people and must be included but that might have no impact on satisfaction or purchase;
• • • It provides an objective way of measuring the uniqueness of each attribute among existing products and/or brands; and
• • • It provides more information about each attribute (2 aspects versus 1).

Disadvantages

• • • It requires 2 ratings, increasing burden on respondent;
• • • Multiplying the 2 measures may not be the best way to combine them (add? weight?); and

• • • There is a temptation to assume that the greater the range, the more "important" the attribute. But the determinance concept merely states that attributes offered at about the same level in all products and/or brands can have little or no leverage for purchase decisions or satisfaction.

One way to analyze respondent ratings is to calculate average scores for each attribute for both importance and the amount of difference among brands. These averages are then plotted on horizontal and vertical axes. An example of this is shown in Figure 3.1.

This particular market research firm recommends that its clients ask respondents to rate both the importance and the "discriminating power" of each attribute (in addition to company performance), because they "need to know just what features differentiate [their] product from [their] competitors'." All of these ratings are combined in a proprietary Competitive Leverage Analysis model that links importance, discriminating power, and company performance. Therefore, the determinance concept suggests that only attributes that are both important *and* discriminating should be rated on an ongoing basis in customer satisfaction surveys.

Laddering

A technique known as "laddering" is perhaps the only one of all the methods discussed here that was developed expressly for marketing research and public opinion polling applications (though it has other applications as well). It is based on Means-End Theory (Gutman 1982; Reynolds, Cockle, and Rochon 1990), which proposes that a hierarchy of values (and hence a hierarchy of attribute importances) exists in each consumer and that this hierarchy can be revealed through a systematic questioning process known as laddering. A laddering study begins with a prescribed series of questions for each respondent, as follows:[3]

1. Ask respondent to elicit attributes that best *distinguish* among groups of similar products/brands/stores, in bipolar format.
2. Ask which pole he or she prefers.
3. Select key attributes to use for laddering.
4. Ask why he or she selected the desired pole.
5. Ask why that pole is important; what are the benefits for respondent?

---

[3]Source: Strategic Assessments Inc., Dallas, Texas.

What's missing from this picture?

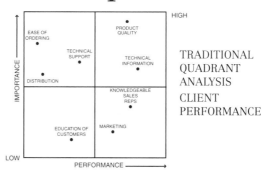

TRADITIONAL
QUADRANT
ANALYSIS

CLIENT
PERFORMANCE

Discriminating Power!

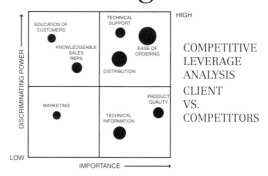

COMPETITIVE
LEVERAGE
ANALYSIS

CLIENT
VS.
COMPETITORS

In traditional quadrant analysis, the characteristics of your product are graphed by importance and performance. The picture may be interesting, but incomplete. Even distorted. A critical dimension measuring the discriminating power of your product is missing. In order to really understand why customers buy what they buy, you need to know just what features differentiate your product from your competitors'.

At Taylor Nelson Sofres Intersearch we have developed a technique that depicts this discriminating power. We call it **Competitive Leverage Analysis or CLA**. Our clients call it "indispensable."

Call today for more information on **CLA**. Find out how our staff of analytical experts can help you make the best use of your data.

6. Continue asking why each chosen benefit is important, as a means of moving respondent "up the ladder of abstraction" to reveal how a specified product and/or service enables respondent to satisfy one or more ultimate personal goals and values.

The following is an example of a simple ladder from one respondent:

Interviewer: "You said you prefer a wine cooler when you get home after work because of the *full-bodied taste*. What's so good about a full-bodied taste after work?"
Respondent: "It feels good to drink something satisfying."
Interviewer: "Why is a satisfying drink important to you after work?"
Respondent: "With coolers, I get filled up and it's easy to stop. Plus, I tend not to eat as much dinner."

The complete sequence of questions led to the following simple ladder:

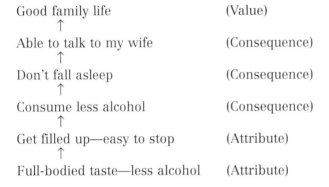

Good family life	(Value)
↑	
Able to talk to my wife	(Consequence)
↑	
Don't fall asleep	(Consequence)
↑	
Consume less alcohol	(Consequence)
↑	
Get filled up—easy to stop	(Attribute)
↑	
Full-bodied taste—less alcohol	(Attribute)

Responses of this kind are input to a special proprietary computer program that aggregates ladders from many respondents to produce a single diagram that shows the sequence and relative frequency of mention of pairs of attributes for different ladders. An example from a study of dog food is shown in Figure 3.2. The more frequently mentioned ladder pairs are marked by heavier lines. The shaded area shows the most frequently mentioned set of ladders.

Advantages

- • • It provides a "structure of values";
- • • It identifies most important motivators;
- • • It is easy for respondent to answer, uses respondent's own terminology; and
- • • Ladders emerge from interviewer–respondent interaction.

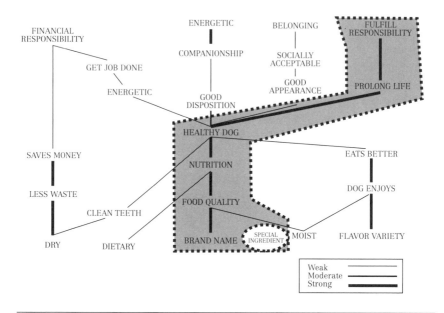

Source: Strategic Assessments Inc., Dallas, Texas.

Disadvantages

• • • It relies on top-of-mind elicitation;

• • • In some situations, ladders cannot be produced;

• • • It requires competent, experienced interviewing to develop a personal style and interaction that can produce ladders; and

• • • It usually requires a long interview (60–75 minutes).

Although a laddering study can be expensive, proponents argue that it reveals insights into consumer values and attribute importances that can be extremely useful. It requires expert professional experience to build and interpret the kinds of ladders in Figure 3.2. However, any researcher can gain insight by asking the series of questions, discussed previously, that are used to produce ladders. This can be a powerful tool for moving consumers "up the ladder of abstraction" that leads to their ultimate goals and values. These have been shown to be the most important motivators of buying behavior (Reynolds, Gutman, and Fiedler 1984; Reynolds and Jamieson 1984), and they are the ones that should be included in customer satisfaction tracking studies.

COMBINATIONS OF DIRECT METHODS

Any of the foregoing direct methods can be used alone, in combination with others, or expanded. For example, laddering starts with a form of elicitation and then asks the direct question, "Why is this important to you?" This, in turn, elicits other important attributes on the way to the most important one(s) at the top of the ladder. In the process, many important hot buttons are uncovered. They are even depicted graphically, in hierarchical order, with at least a rough indication of their relative importance as they move from the bottom of the ladder to the top.

Another interesting example of using a combination of methods is known as a "quality profile," illustrated by Gale in his book, *Managing Customer Value* (1994). Respondents (alone or in groups) are asked to name the *most important attributes* about a specific product and/or service (elicitation method). Then, they are told to allocate 100 points among these attributes to indicate their relative importance (constant sum method). Next, they are asked to rate the *performance* of the sponsoring company on each attribute using a 10-point scale. Finally, they rate a specific competitor, or all major competitors combined, on the same attributes and scales. An example from a study of frying chickens purchased in supermarkets is shown in Table 3.4 (Gale 1994, p. 33).

The important quality attributes elicited from respondents are shown in Column 1. Columns 2, 3, and 4 show the weights and performance ratings for each attribute for both Perdue chickens and the competition. Gale then calculates a ratio of Perdue chicken ratings to those of the competition (Column 5) on each attribute and weights these ratios by the constant sum importance values (Column 6). These values are summed across all attributes to produce an overall weighted quality index. Anything higher than 100 shows how much better Perdue chickens are than the competition (in this case, 26.1%) and the converse for anything lower. He calls this the "market-perceived quality ratio."

Gale then goes on to create a "customer value map" by plotting this quality ratio versus the actual relative price for both Perdue chickens and the competition, as is shown in Figure 3.3. Then a fair-value line is entered to indicate where relative perceived quality is equal to relative price. In this graph, Perdue chickens are above the fair-value line, indicating a superior value, and other chickens are shown to be below. Even though Perdue chickens cost more, they are shown to be

▼ TABLE 3.4 QUALITY PROFILE: CHICKEN BUSINESS, AFTER FRANK PERDUE

Performance Scores

Quality Attributes 1	Weight 2	Perdue 3	Avg. Comp. 4	Ratio 5 = 3/4	Weight times Ratio 6 = 2 × 5
Yellow bird	10	8.1	7.2	1.13	11.3
Meat-to-bone	20	9.0	7.3	1.23	24.6
No pinfeathers	20	9.2	6.5	1.42	28.4
Fresh	15	8.0	8.0	1.00	15.0
Availability	10	8.0	8.0	1.00	10.0
Brand image	25	9.4	6.4	1.47	36.8
	100				126.1

Customer satisfaction: 8.8   7.1

Market-perceived quality ratio:

Adapted with permission of The Free Press from *The PIMS Principles*, by Robert D. Buzzell and Bradley T. Gale; copyright © 1978 by The Free Press.

a superior value by the customer value map. This is a useful technique that any company can apply.

SUMMARY

Most of the direct methods for measuring attribute importance are simple and easy to execute (aside from laddering), even for people with little or no training in statistical analysis. They also have great intuitive appeal and therefore are usually acceptable to both management and employees whose performance is being evaluated based, in part, on the CSM program. For these reasons, direct methods of measuring attribute importance are popular and widely used for customer satisfaction studies, as well as for marketing research and public opinion polling, especially by those who have the least experience in statistical analysis.

However, because of the disadvantages and limitations of most direct approaches, mentioned previously for each technique, many experienced research professionals prefer one or more of the indirect

▼ FIGURE 3.3 CUSTOMER VALUE MAP: CHICKEN BUSINESS

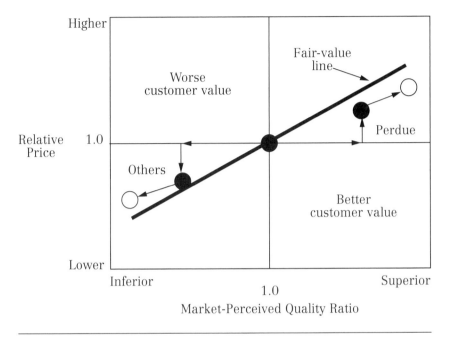

Source: Gale, Bradley T. (1994), *Managing Customer Value: Creating Quality and Service that Customers Can See*. New York: The Free Press. © 1994, Bradley T. Gale.

methods discussed in the next two chapters. The next chapter begins by summarizing the various problems with direct methods and then discusses one especially useful class of indirect methods that is based on regression analysis. Then we demonstrate a way to combine both direct and indirect results for each attribute and thereby take advantage of information contained in both approaches.

REFERENCES

Aaker, David A., V. Kumar, and George S. Day (1998), *Marketing Research*. New York: John Wiley & Sons, Inc.

Alpert, Mark I. (1971), "Identification of Determinant Attributes—A Comparison of Methods," *Journal of Marketing Research*, 8 (May), 184–91.

Foote, N.N. (1961), *Consumer Behavior: Household Decision-Making*, Vol. 4. New York: New York University Press.

Gale, Bradley T. (1994), *Managing Customer Value: Creating Quality and Service that Customers Can See*. New York: The Free Press.

Green, Paul E. and Donald S. Tull (1978), *Research for Marketing Decisions*, 4th ed. Englewood Cliffs, NJ: Prentice Hall.

Griffin, Abbie and John R. Hauser (1993), "The Voice of the Customer," *Marketing Science*, 12 (Winter), 1–26.

Gutman, J. (1982), "A Means-End Chain Model Based on Consumer Categorization Processes," *Journal of Marketing*, 46 (2), 60–72.

Heeler, Roger M., Chike Okechuku, and Stan Reid (1979), "Attribute Importance: Contrasting Measurements," *Journal of Marketing Research*, 8 (August), 291–97.

Jaccard, James, David Brinberg, and Lee J. Ackerman (1986), Assessing Attribute Importance: A Comparison of Six Methods," *Journal of Consumer Research*, 12 (March), 463–68.

Myers, James H. and Mark I. Alpert (1968), "Determinant Buying Attributes: Meaning and Measurement," *Journal of Marketing*, 32 (October), 13–20.

Reynolds, Thomas J., B. Cockle, and J. Rochon (1990), "The Strategic Imperatives of Advertising: Implications of Means-End Theory and Research Findings," *Canadian Journal of Marketing Research*, 9, 3–13.

———, Jonathan Gutman, and J. Fiedler (1984), "Understanding Consumers' Cognitive Structures: The Relationship of Levels of Abstraction to Judgments of Psychological Distance and Preference," in *Psychological Processes of Advertising Effects: Theory, Research, and Application*, A. Mitchell and L. Alwitt, eds. Hillsdale, NJ: Lawrence Erlbaum Associates.

——— and L. Jamieson (1984), "Image Representations: An Analytical Framework," in *Perceived Quality of Products, Services, and Stores*, Jack Jacoby and Jerry Olson, eds. Lexington, MA: Lexington Books.

CHAPTER 4

INDIRECT METHODS OF MEASURING ATTRIBUTE IMPORTANCE: REGRESSION-BASED

In this chapter, we focus on what are probably the 3 most widely used *indirect* methods for measuring attribute importance:

- • • correlation/regression,
- • • conjoint analysis (full profile), and
- • • conjoint analysis (pairwise trade-offs).

The next chapter presents several other indirect methods that might be useful in some specific applications. Although indirect techniques may be more accurate in some ways than the direct methods in the prior chapter, most are more difficult to apply. Several require a good knowledge of statistical analysis tools and techniques, which is usually available in a company's market research department or from outside suppliers.

In contrast to the transparent direct methods, in which respondents know they are being asked about attribute importance, indirect methods might be called "opaque." In some of these methods, respondents probably have no idea that they are indicating the relative importance of the specific product and/or service attributes they are using or rating in one way or another. In other indirect methods, they might know that they are basing their overall preferences on several attributes but be unaware that a primary objective is to determine the relative importance of each attribute. Why would anyone want to use opaque indirect measures rather than transparent direct measures?

PROBLEMS WITH DIRECT METHODS

Direct methods are based on the assumption that if you want to know what is important to people, you should just ask them. We assume that most people are logical and rational, and they know what influences them and what they want. However, a great deal of survey research experience and experimentation over the years has revealed many reasons why respondents cannot always be relied on to give accurate *and* useful answers, even though they might fully intend to do so. Most of these reasons are well known and discussed in texts on survey research and public opinion polling. Others were discovered in the experience of this writer and other survey researchers. Here is a recap of several potential problems, most of which were mentioned in Chapter 3 as disadvantages of each of the direct methods.

Inability of respondent to answer. In some cases, people simply do not know the extent to which they are influenced by a particular attribute or feature. They sometimes understate or underestimate the importance of such aspects as styling or design characteristics, or they forget experiences with, or certain attributes of, a product or service, all of which can affect their choices. They may not remember what price they paid for a certain household item or how many times they went to the movies last year, for example.

Unwillingness of respondent to answer. Sometimes respondents know that a particular attribute is important but are reluctant to admit this to themselves or others. Again, this can involve styling or design attributes, but it can also include anything other than the functional attributes of a product and/or service that are considered "sensible." Also included in these potential problems are aspects other than product and/or service attributes, such as peer pressures (buying a BMW or a sport utility vehicle because friends own one), family pressures, or pressure from a salesperson.

Overemphasis on sensible attributes. Time and again, respondents overstate the importance of such intrinsically desirable attributes as personal safety, low price, convenience, and so forth. Of course, these are important attributes, especially for certain products and/or services. But many times, researchers have found much higher importance levels for these items using *direct* rather than *indirect* methods, which suggests that respondents may be exaggerating their importance because they believe this is what they ought to think, that is, what sensible, logical persons (like themselves) would naturally think.

Playback of advertising copy points. As mentioned previously, advertising agencies have found that people often play back copy claims when they are asked what product and/or service attributes are especially important. These may or may not be the attributes that are actually most important to them, but they are the ones people remember from advertising and are a convenient way to get through a survey interview quickly.

Everything is important. Table 3.1 in Chapter 3 clearly shows how a sample of respondents could rate so many attributes so high in importance that they provided little guidance for management of a utility company. This phenomenon is often found, especially in the case of complex products and/or services or for those that are especially important to people.

High importance but little effect on preference. As was pointed out in Chapter 3, some attributes that are rated highly can actually be of critical importance to respondents, yet they make *little or no difference in terms of preference or choice.* This is because every other competing product is perceived to be delivering that attribute or benefit to approximately the same degree. Examples include car engines that start first thing on a cold morning, safety in airline travel, and the safety of money in banks. Whenever all of the major competitors are perceived to be offering these important attributes or benefits equally, they probably have little or no impact on preference or choice.

For all of these reasons (and possibly others as well), many experienced survey researchers increasingly have come to rely on indirect methods of measuring attribute importance. They believe these methods eliminate or greatly reduce most of the problems of direct methods, leading to more accurate measurement. Another real advantage to indirect methods is that, by definition, respondents are not asked to spend time rating or indicating attribute importance. This often means that an entire set of attribute ratings (i.e., importance ratings) can be eliminated, with considerable savings of both time and cost!

CORRELATION/REGRESSION ANALYSIS

The best place to start for understanding indirect methods is with correlation/regression analysis. The basic principles of regression are the foundation for most indirect methods, and an understanding of this technique will show how attribute importance can be inferred or implied from the way the analysis is carried out. Regression analysis is used in all 3 of the indirect methods discussed here (correlation/regression, full-profile conjoint, pairwise trade-off conjoint) to determine attribute importance, so it is important to understand its conceptual foundations.

For readers not familiar with regression analysis, the term "regression" is used to refer to the situation in which the values of one variable or attribute are to be predicted from the values of another variable or variables (see Churchill 1995, Ch. 16). A regression "model" or formula shows how this prediction is to be performed for any specified attribute or set of attributes. It also shows the *form* of the relationship(s). In contrast, the term "correlation" refers to the *degree* of relationship between any two variables or set of variables. Regression and correlation are opposite sides of the same coin. In the present context, we are especially interested in correlation analysis. We assume that the higher the correlation between two variables, the more important one is in understanding or affecting the other. Therefore, the higher the correlation between a company attribute and overall satisfaction or intention to switch, the more important it is to respondents. This is an assumption, because correlation does not prove causation, but many researchers think it is a reasonable one for most survey research applications.

Correlation/regression typically analyzes *performance* (not importance) ratings given by respondents when they are asked to rate or evaluate some existing products, services, or companies on several attributes. Ratings of this kind are very common in marketing research surveys, so the data required for this method are already available in many studies.

In customer satisfaction research, respondents are often asked to rate the performance of one or more companies on several selected attributes. They must also provide an overall evaluation of some kind for each company (e.g., overall satisfaction, likelihood of switching). Then, the relative importance of each attribute is determined by calculating a coefficient of correlation (r) between performance ratings and overall ratings. The size of this coefficient reflects the amount of variation in one variable that can be explained by the other variable; the higher the coefficient for a given attribute, the more influence it is *presumed* (but not proven) to have on overall satisfaction.

▼ FIGURE 4.1 INFERRED IMPORTANCE: WEAK

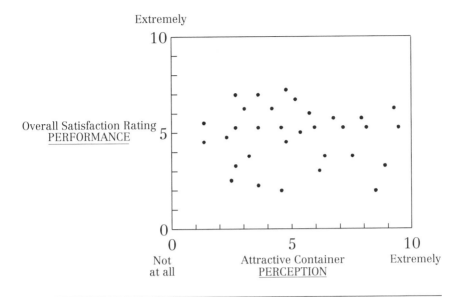

Figures 4.1 and 4.2 show how correlation analysis works in the case of hypothetical ratings for several brands of a hair shampoo for women. Each dot represents one respondent. Figure 4.1 shows that, as performance ratings increase on "attractive container," overall satisfaction ratings remain approximately the same; they do not increase. The resulting correlation would be approximately 0.0, and we would assume or infer that the containers' attractiveness has little or no effect on overall satisfaction with the shampoo. In Figure 4.2, in contrast, as ratings increase on "cleans the hair," they increase correspondingly on overall satisfaction. The correlation here might be approximately 0.7–0.8. Therefore, *the higher the correlation, the more highly related the two sets of ratings are* and the more likely we are to infer or assume that a particular attribute influences or drives overall satisfaction. (Correlation coefficients can range from +1.0 to 0.0 to –1.0; ±1.0 are the highest possible coefficients, and they indicate a perfect positive or negative relationship—something seldom found in the real world of survey research!)[1]

---

[1]The relationship between the two variables must be "linear" (i.e., fit a *straight* line) for the kind of correlation usually calculated (Pearson, zero-order). All of our discussions apply only to this type of relationship.

▼ FIGURE 4.2 INFERRED IMPORTANCE: STRONG

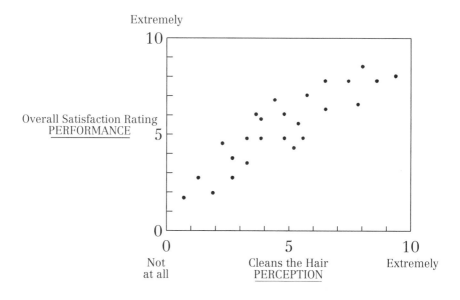

Table 4.1 provides an excellent comparison of the results obtained by applying an indirect method (correlation analysis) and a direct method (average importance ratings) to the same data from the same respondents. The average importance ratings in the first column are exactly the same as in Table 3.1. The numbers in the second column are correlation coefficients (squared) that show the percentage of the variation in overall satisfaction ratings that is explained or accounted for by each attribute separately. Now, if these two columns of numbers were in the same rank order, there would be no need for an indirect measure of importance. Both methods would be producing the same results. That they are not is typical, and this shows how indirect methods can provide a very different perspective on attribute importance than direct methods do. This is almost always the case.

Note that the attribute with the highest correlation with overall satisfaction is "Treats me like a valued customer," but it is only around the middle on the basis of mean importance ratings. Conversely, the 6 attributes with the highest importance ratings are in the lower middle in terms of correlated importance. For these data then, direct and indirect methods clearly produce quite different results. These findings surprised the management of this utility. The company decided to focus on correlated rather than rated importance and assembled an in-

▼ TABLE 4.1 COMPARISON OF STATED AND INFERRED IMPORTANCE OF UTILITY PROGRAMS AND ACTIVITIES

Activities	Mean Importance Rating	Correlation (r^2)
Top importance activities		
Effectively handles emergencies	9.79	7%
Maintains reliable source of energy	9.76	8
Does the job right the first time	9.74	10
Restores service quickly	9.72	8
Accurate meter reading and billing	9.69	8
Competent and well-trained employees	9.69	8
Resolves problems quickly	9.68	11
Relatively stable rates	9.66	13
Tries to keep rates low	9.66	16
Provides consistent energy	9.65	5
Provides safety information	9.63	8
Plans effectively for the future	9.60	14
Takes steps to not harm the environment	9.60	11
Cost-conscious	9.59	16
Provides safety checks	9.59	7
Middle-range importance activities		
Makes service calls at convenient hours	9.48	7
Treats customers as if valued	9.42	19
Programs to help seniors and low-income customers	9.29	8
Convenient hours to call	9.28	4
Polite and courteous employees	9.26	13
Offers programs to help control costs	9.20	9
Provides appliance adjustments and relights	9.20	9
Keeps customers well-informed	9.06	9
Answers phone promptly	9.06	9
Efficient in number of employees	9.04	5
Lower-range importance activities		
Offers optional rate plans	8.91	11
Involved with local community	8.80	13
Convenient office hours	8.37	5
Convenient office locations	8.10	6
Contributes money to worthy causes	7.96	10

ternal task force to determine what exactly makes customers feel that they are "valued."

Advantages

- • • It does not rely on respondents' stated importance,
- • • It is an easy task for respondents,
- • • Analysis is relatively simple using a PC and appropriate software, and
- • • It usually provides much greater range of attribute importance than importance ratings.

Disadvantages

- • • Correlation is not causation, can't be certain of results;
- • • It is not usually possible at individual respondent level;
- • • Correlations across total sample can obscure distinct preference segments, therefore, best to segment first; and
- • • Multiple regression coefficients can be distorted if collinearity among attributes is high (as it often is).

In summary, this method is considered by many a powerful way of finding out what really influences people, and it eliminates many of the problems inherent in direct methods. Anyone with a minimal statistical capability can calculate correlation coefficients using a PC and appropriate software (e.g., SPSS, SAS, BMD, Excel, SYSTAT). More and more companies have come to rely on correlation analysis in one form or another for measuring attribute importance.

A Caveat

A note of caution is in order when using the correlation/regression analysis method. The preceding discussion is based primarily on *simple* correlation, in which each attribute is correlated separately against an overall satisfaction measure. However, because it is usually the case that many attributes are being rated in a customer satisfaction study, some analysts are tempted to use *multiple* correlation/regression because it can process large numbers of attributes in one pass through the computer. The problem here is that multiple regression coefficients can be very misleading, because one attribute will get a high regression coefficient while a very similar one will get a much lower coefficient (this avoids overweighting the basic idea behind the similar attributes). An example of this is shown in Chapter 10.

The usual solutions are to (1) eliminate attributes that are highly similar to others, (2) develop "factor scores" that summarize the basic idea into a single weighted score, or (3) do simple regressions/correlations of each attribute separately, as was shown previously. The choice among these is difficult and requires a good knowledge of statistical analysis techniques.

As an aside, it is interesting to note how much controversy there is about the desirability of inferring attribute importance from either correlation or regression analysis, even among experienced market researchers and professional statistical analysts. One experienced analyst recently commented:

> A higher correlation means more joint variance is shared, period. Usually, but not universally, if you rank the independent attributes by their correlation with the dependent variable and again by their own variance, you will find that the two lists agree quite well, that is, have a statistically significant rank order correlation coefficient. My contention, then, is that by using correlation as a measure of "derived" importance, you are not doing much other than using the variance of the scales themselves as measures of importance. There are certainly exceptions, but there are many, many cases where it's so.[2]

CONJOINT ANALYSIS (FULL PROFILE)

One of the most popular high-tech research techniques in use today is known as "conjoint analysis," often referred to as "trade-off analysis." It is based on complex research designs that provide a wide range of benefits for users (for a review, see Green and Srinivasan 1990). Here, we are interested in only one of those benefits: measuring attribute importance. There are two distinctly different approaches to conjoint analysis—full profile and pairwise trade-offs.[3] In this section, we discuss only the first of these, full-profile conjoint analysis.

In the usual format, respondents are asked to rate or rank approximately 10 to 20 *hypothetical* products and/or services in terms of overall preference to them. Each product and/or service "profile" (i.e., composition) is constructed by the analyst using 4 to 8 relatively independent attributes with 2 to 5 objective (clearly defined) levels for each. These hypothetical products are constructed in such a way that the attributes are *not related* across the profiles; that is, none of the

---

[2]Comment by Gary Mullet, Gary Mullet & Associates.
[3]Choice and discrete choice conjoint models can also be used, but these are even more complex, and most of them produce importance values for each attribute only at the aggregate level, not for each individual respondent.

▼**FIGURE 4.3 FULL-PROFILE RANKINGS FOR AIRLINE TRAVEL OPTIONS**

Example: Please rank the following in terms of preference.

Airline	Service	Departure Time	Round Trip	Rank
Northwest	Nonstop	Midday	$260	____
Continental	1-stop or connect +1-2 hrs. (w/restr)	Midday	$325	____
Western	1-stop or connect +1-2 hrs. (w/restr)	Morning	$275	____
United	Nonstop (w/restr)	Evening	$250	____
Northwest	Nonstop (w/restr)	Afternoon	$400	____
Continental	1-stop (w/restr)	Afternoon	$300	____
United	Nonstop	Morning	$450	____
Western	1-stop or connect +1-2 hrs.	Evening	$350	____

profiles is similar to any of the others. An example of this is shown in Figure 4.3 using a proprietary study conducted by a major U.S. airline. Each row is a hypothetical airline trip (a profile). If these profiles are not constructed properly, it would not be possible to estimate the importance of each attribute. (A preanalysis is sometimes necessary to ensure this.)

Using the preference rankings given by respondents, a computer calculates the relative importance (called "utility") of each *level* of each attribute, and from these utilities, the relative importance of each attribute can easily be calculated.[4] The basic procedure for obtaining

[4]This is achieved by subtracting the lowest from the highest utility value for each attribute for each respondent. The larger the difference, the more important the attribute is. But this can lead to problems. If two respondents ranked the profiles in exactly the *opposite* fashion, their calculated importances would be exactly the same, even though their preferences were completely opposite. Therefore, the direction of attribute utilities must be considered in every case (comment by Gary Mullet, Gary Mullet & Associates).

utilities is regression analysis, the same method as was used in the previous section on correlation/regression. It analyzes the relationship between attribute levels and overall evaluations across all product and/or service profiles. In conjoint analysis, respondents simply provide overall ratings or rankings. They are not required to rate the performance levels of the attributes because they are already known from the composition of the profiles. Utilities usually can be calculated for each respondent separately, as well as for all respondents combined.

An example will help illustrate. In Figure 4.3, there are 4 possible departure times: morning, midday, afternoon, and evening. Suppose the computer calculates the following utility values for each of these (utilities can range from 0 to 1.0) for Respondent 1:

• • • Morning (9),
• • • Midday (5),
• • • Afternoon (4), and
• • • Evening (1).

The relative importance of departure time is calculated by subtracting the lowest from the highest utility value: $9 - 1 = 8$. This value is compared with corresponding values for the other 3 factors to determine the *relative influence of each factor on trip schedule preference*. If the calculated importance values for the other 3 factors range from, say, 7 down to 2 or 3, then, for this respondent, departure time would be the most important factor. A price-conscious respondent would have the highest calculated importance value for trip cost, of course.

Thus, full-profile conjoint analysis provides not only the relative importance of each attribute as a whole, but also the value to the respondent of each level or characteristic within each attribute. This makes it possible for a computer to calculate the overall value of every possible combination of levels across all attributes and to put these in rank order of overall preference. As just mentioned, this can be done for each respondent separately, as well as for all respondents combined. In this way, the ideal product or service package can be identified.

Advantages

• • • It forces trade-offs, respondent cannot have all best levels;
• • • Researcher can obtain overall attribute importances by indirect means for each respondent with some precision;
• • • Researcher can obtain utilities for each level of each attribute for each respondent; and

• • Researcher can segment market on the basis of patterns of attribute importance for each respondent to obtain "importance segments."

Disadvantages

• • • It is best when attribute levels are objective and not judgmental,
• • • It is difficult to construct properly the hypothetical arrays to be rated or ranked, and
• • • It *is usually* difficult for respondent to absorb and compare accurately 15 to 18 arrays with 3 to 8 attribute levels in each.

Note that a major advantage of conjoint over correlation/regression analysis is that attribute importances can be obtained for each respondent separately using an indirect method. This makes it possible to segment a market on the basis of the attributes or product and/or service features that respondents believe are most important, without the potential problems involved in asking them directly. In turn, this makes it possible to estimate market share for each of several existing or proposed new products or product profiles using the utilities calculated for each level of each company attribute. These and other capabilities make full-profile conjoint analysis a very powerful and popular research technique.

CONJOINT ANALYSIS (PAIRWISE TRADE-OFFS)

A different approach to conjoint analysis is known as "pairwise trade-offs." In its simplest form, it presents respondents with all possible combinations of levels of 2 attributes at a time (hence, pairwise) across all possible pairs of attributes. Respondents are asked to rate or rank all combinations of levels in terms of their preference. Figure 4.4 shows a hypothetical example of this for passenger automobiles. This respondent has given a rank of 1 to a car with a top speed of 130 mph and a low price of $8,000. No surprise here. But the rank of 2 tells us that he or she is willing to give up a higher top speed to keep the price at $8000. Thus, price is more important than top speed—a trade-off.

These rankings then become the dependent variables for a multiple regression analysis that calculates the relative importance of each level of each factor (top speed, price, etc.). This is the same statistical analysis technique used in the full-profile version of conjoint analysis, and the outcome is usually quite comparable, even though the input format is very different. Thus, both forms of conjoint analysis are in-

	Top Speed			Seating Capacity			Months of Warranty	
	130	100	70	2	4	6	60	12
Price								
$ 8,000	1	2	5	2	1	3	1	3
$10,000	3	4	6	5	4	6	2	5
$12,000	7	8	9	8	7	9	7	8
Top Speed								
130 mph				2	1	3	1	2
100 mph				5	4	6	3	4
70 mph				8	7	9	7	8
Seating Capacity								
2							3	5
4							1	4
6							3	6

Adapted from Richard M. Johnson (1974), "Trade-off Analysis of Customer Values," *Journal of Marketing Research*, 11 (May), 121–29.

direct methods of measuring attribute importance based on correlation/regression analysis.

In practice, the complete pairwise trade-off matrix in Figure 4.4 is seldom used because it is so cumbersome. Instead, a format similar to the one in Figure 4.5 provides a simpler task for respondents. This example shows how all attributes of a personal computer are traded off against different price levels. Respondents indicate which of the 2 pairs they would choose and how strongly they prefer the chosen al-

▼ FIGURE 4.5 PAIRWISE ANALYSIS OF COMPUTER ATTRIBUTES

Warranty length is the amount of time from delivery that the computer is covered by a warranty that pays for repairs.

The levels are: 90 days, and
　　　　　　　　1 year.

Warranty Length:	1 year	-OR-	90 days
Price Per Computer:	$price + $75		$price
	Strongly prefer left	Equal preference	Strongly prefer right
	L4　　L3　　L2　　L1	0	R1　　R2　　R3　　R4

Time to product availability is the time from when the computer is ordered to when it is received.

The levels are: 30 business days, and
　　　　　　　　5 business days.

Time to Product Availability:	5 business days	-OR-	30 business days
Price Per Computer:	$price + $250		$price
	Strongly prefer left	Equal preference	Strongly prefer right
	L4　　L3　　L2　　L1	0	R1　　R2　　R3　　R4

Reputation for on-time delivery reflects the typical delivery performance of the purchase source. Some sources always deliver when they say they will. Others sometimes deliver 5 to 10 days later than they promise.

The levels are: Sometimes 5 to 10 days late, and
　　　　　　　　Always on time.

Reputation for On-Time Delivery:	Sometimes 5 to 10 days late	-OR-	Always on time
Price Per Computer:	$price		$price + $175
	Strongly prefer left	Equal preference	Strongly prefer right
	L4　　L3　　L2　　L1	0	R1　　R2　　R3　　R4

ternative. Then, all other nonprice attributes are traded off against one another, in pairs.

Sometimes each component of a pair contains 3 attributes, and the pairs are constructed in such a way that all levels appear an equal number of times. The choices are the dependent variables, regression is used to determine the utility values for attribute levels, and importance is calculated by subtracting the lowest from the highest utilities for each attribute.

Probably the most widely used technique for pairwise trade-offs is known as Adaptive Conjoint Analysis, by Sawtooth Software. Respondents are guided through the trade-off process by computer. They respond by punching appropriate keys for each task, as instructed by the computer. This technique can handle many more variables than full-profile conjoint, but respondents must indicate which of up to 30 or more attributes are the most important to them. These are then traded off against each other. This is a modification of the original pairwise trade-off matrix, and it involves both direct (selection of attributes) and indirect (pairwise trade-offs) approaches to determining attribute importance.

Advantages

- • • It forces trade-offs directly between pairs of attributes,
- • • Researcher can obtain indirect importances of both attributes and levels for each respondent, and
- • • Researcher can use results to segment market on the basis of patterns of attribute importance for each respondent.

Disadvantages

- • • It is best when attribute levels are objective and not judgmental;
- • • It considers only pairs of attributes, therefore assumes ceteris paribus (other things being equal); and
- • • Relatively few attributes can be traded off directly.

Both types of conjoint analysis have the advantage in that they can (1) measure attribute importance (2) using an indirect method (3) at the individual respondent level. It is this last characteristic that gives conjoint analysis a distinct advantage over correlation/regression analysis. The latter can usually be done only at the aggregate level, pooled across a sample of respondents. Because of this, both forms of conjoint analysis provide a means of segmenting the market on the basis of the relative importance of attributes to respondents. This leads to other important advantages too complex to discuss here (including the prediction of market share for a new or modified product and/or service).

REFERENCES

Churchill, Gilbert A., Jr. (1995), *Marketing Research: Methodological Foundations*, 6th ed. Hinsdale, IL: The Dryden Press.

Green, Paul E. and V. Srinivasan (1990), "Conjoint Analysis in Marketing: New Developments with Implications for Research and Practice," *Journal of Marketing*, 54 (October), 3–19.

Johnson, Richard M. (1974), "Trade-off Analysis of Customer Values," *Journal of Marketing Research*, 11 (May), 121–29.

CHAPTER 5

OTHER INDIRECT METHODS OF MEASURING ATTRIBUTE IMPORTANCE

There are several other indirect methods of measuring attribute importance in addition to those based on correlation/ regression analysis, as described in the previous chapter. The most useful of these are presented here. Although none of them will be as applicable or widely used as those based on regression, they do offer alternatives that might be appropriate for specific applications. At the very least, they help show how many different approaches have been developed to measure the relative importance of attributes and why it is impossible to select the single most accurate one for every application.

The following techniques are discussed in this chapter:

• • • Extreme differences,
• • • Subjective probabilities,
• • • Indifference level,
• • • Information display board,
• • • Computer content analysis (semiotics), and
• • • Strategic cube analysis.

In the next chapter, a number of studies are presented that compare results from several methods, both direct and indirect, when applied to the same task and using the same respondents.

METHODS

Extreme Differences

As was noted previously, correlation/regression analysis has the disadvantage that attribute importance usually can be calculated only at the aggregate level, with all respondents combined. Conjoint methods can do this at the individual respondent level, but they do best with only a few attributes that have specific, objectively defined levels. However, sometimes there is a need for an indirect method of measuring attribute importance for *each respondent separately* for large numbers of attributes that require subjective ratings. The extreme differences method offers a means of accomplishing this rather simply for most product and/or service categories.

With this method, respondents are first asked to name their *most* and *least* preferred brands or companies in a particular product and/or service category among brands and/or companies they know well enough to rate. They are asked to rate these two brands on any number of attributes (e.g., 50–100 or more), using 7- to 10-point scales. Then, for each attribute, the lowest rating (that for the least preferred brand) is subtracted from the highest (that for the most preferred brand) for each respondent separately. The size of these difference scores (absolute, not algebraic) reflects the relative importance of each attribute to each respondent. An example from a proprietary study will help illustrate:

> Please tell us which brand of canned cat food you *most* prefer (or buy most often). Which brand do you *least* prefer (or are least likely to buy)? Now, please rate each of these brands on the following attributes, using a 10-point scale (10 = Describes extremely well, 1 = Does not describe at all well).

Here is a hypothetical analysis for a single respondent who was asked to give ratings on a 10-point scale:

Attribute	Ratings		
	Most	Least	Difference
Cat eats it with relish	10	4	+6
Contains all nutrients cat needs	9	7	+2
Easy to store leftovers	7	7	0

In this example, we can infer that a difference score as large as +6 suggests that "Cat eats it with relish" is much more important than "Easy to store leftovers," which has a 0 difference score, and that "nutrients" is somewhere in between. (The actual study asked respondents to rate nearly 100 attributes of canned cat foods.) The logic is that, if there is no difference between the most and least preferred brands in terms of storing leftovers, this is not likely to be an attribute that drives the overall desirability of a canned cat food to any meaningful extent. Conversely, the greater the difference in ratings, the more likely it is that an attribute affects overall evaluations or choice.

Advantages

- • • It is a simplified way to obtain attribute importance for each respondent,
- • • It can be used for large numbers of attributes (as compared with conjoint), and
- • • Attributes need not have objective levels (versus conjoint).

Disadvantages

- • • Two data points for each attribute might not be stable (i.e., reliable),
- • • Respondents need to give 2 sets of ratings, and
- • • Most or least preferred brand sometimes can be difficult for respondent to select.

The method of extreme differences offers an alternative when a researcher (1) wants to segment a market in terms of the benefits desired, (2) has a large number of attributes that are (3) rated on a subjective basis, and (4) wants an indirect method of measuring attribute importance. However, we should note that its statistical properties and stability are weaker than those of the three indirect methods discussed previously. For this reason, the method should be used with some caution, though this writer has used it successfully on several occasions.

Subjective Probabilities

The subjective probabilities method presents respondents with 2 statements that differ only on the level of a single attribute. Respondents are asked to estimate the probability that they would be willing to consider buying an object with and without this attribute. The absolute difference between these 2 probabilities is used as the measure of importance. For example (Jaccard, Brinberg, and Ackerman 1986, pp. 465–466),

> Suppose that a particular car was *inexpensive*. How willing would you be to consider this as a car you might buy?
> Suppose that a particular car was *expensive*. How willing would you be to consider this as a car you might buy?

  12-point scale:
    11 = Very willing to consider it.
     0 = Not at all willing to consider it.

If a respondent gave a rating of 9 for a car that was inexpensive and 2 for one that was expensive, this would produce an importance weight of 7 for car expense or cost. Similar questions would be used for other attributes.

Advantages

• • • Respondent task is easy to understand;
• • • Subjective probabilities are given in terms of estimated purchase or choice, not just preference; and
• • • It gives attribute importance at the individual level.

Disadvantages

• • • Attribute descriptions may lack clarity (e.g., how expensive is "expensive"?),
• • • It is not easy to accommodate attributes that are lengthy or have complex descriptions, and
• • • Context is not very realistic.

The subjective probabilities method seems most useful when there are small numbers of attributes that can be described in a word or two. The basic principle is similar to that of the extreme differences method, but here, the extremes are in terms of a single attribute rather than most and least favorite brands. In both cases, the relationship, and therefore importance, is inferred from only 2 data points, so results may be less stable than for other methods.

Indifference Level

Another indirect method that could be useful in some applications is known as "indifference level." Respondents are presented with brief feature profiles of 2 products or brands of the same type. All features or attribute levels are the same with the following exceptions: For 1 attribute, 1 brand has a higher level, which indicates a more desirable amount than the other. The other attribute has a specified level for 1 brand but a blank for the other. The respondent is asked to fill in the blank with the level or amount that would make him or her indifferent between the products or brands.

For example,

Consider the following 2 cars and indicate the level of fuel consumption for Car 2 that would result in both cars being of equal value or preference for you.

	Model 1	Model 2
Maximum speed	100 mph	100 mph
Comfort	Good	Good
Price	$12,000	$15,000
Fuel consumption	28 mpg	?

The greater the difference between the 2 fuel consumption amounts, the more important this attribute is. In this example, 1 of the 2 attributes happens to be price. When this is the case, the value of the change in the other attribute can be expressed in terms of dollars (known as a "dollar-metric"). Thus, if a respondent answered 35 mpg, we would know that an increase of 7 mpg is worth $3,000 to him or her. Alternatively, we could ask the interviewer to respond to different mileage amounts, or any other attributes, in terms of dollars. Either approach enables a company to indicate the importance of any attribute on a common scale that is especially meaningful.

Advantages

• • • It forces limited trade-offs among especially important attributes,
• • • Respondent can choose any amount for indifference level, and
• • • Task is rather realistic and easily understood.

Disadvantages

• • • There is only a limited number of attributes for brand profiles,
• • • It takes time to develop all profiles and indifference levels, and
• • • It works best with objective levels of attributes.

Indifference level bears some similarity to pairwise conjoint analysis, in the sense that it forces trade-offs between 2 attributes at a time. It might be considered a special case of the latter without the complexity and power of conjoint models. Often, the most important trade-offs in any application are those versus price. When this is the case, the indifference method might offer a simplified approach to determining the relative importance of all attributes or features other than price through calibration in terms of price, without having to trade off all the attributes against one other. At least it offers an option.

Information Display Board

As its name implies, this technique presents the respondent with a board (perhaps 2 feet × 3 feet) that contains information about a limited number of attributes of a product, service, or company that are judged a priori to be important to the respondent. Detailed information about each of these attributes is provided in the form of stacks of 3 × 5 cards, a separate stack for each attribute. The cards are face down, and each attribute pile is clearly labeled. Each card contains detailed information about a specific aspect of the selected attribute, with comparisons among the companies (e.g., price, discounts, terms of payment for each company). Respondents are asked to choose between 2 or more hypothetical companies or brands to which they might want to give their business. They are told that detailed information about each is contained on the 3 × 5 cards on the information display board.

Respondents then proceed to draw one card after another until they believe they have enough specific information to make their decision. There are no restrictions on how many cards they turn over or the order in which this is completed. Then, the relative importance of each attribute to each respondent can be inferred in 2 separate ways:

• • • the *number* of cards selected for each attribute or
• • • the *order* in which the cards were selected, across and within attributes.

The more cards selected for a given attribute, the more important that attribute is assumed to be. Similarly, attributes whose cards are selected early are likely to be more important than those selected later. These are assumptions, of course, but they seem reasonable. The following example (Lehman and Moore 1980) will illustrate:

In one study, respondents were asked to choose 1 of 5 brands of bread from a small health-food bakery. Half the subjects were given descriptive brand names (e.g., Whole Wheat, Date Bran, Five Grain), the other half were given nondescriptive names (e.g., Soft Sunset, Morning Glow, Bona Flora). Respondents could ask for information on several attributes (e.g., brand name, price, physical product, grains, sweeteners, last date bread can be sold, estimated calories). Information had to be acquired one piece (i.e., attribute) at a time, and any piece could be acquired as many times as desired and in any order.

Advantages

- • • Task setting seems realistic to respondents,
- • • Importance is inferred from behavior, and
- • • Different measures of importance can be tried and validated.

Disadvantages

- • • It requires a laboratory-type setting;
- • • It is difficult to operationalize;
- • • It monitors only external acquisition, not internal processing of information; and
- • • There is little or no validation of this technique, especially in commercial settings.

Note that this is the only method that requires the respondent to do something. Importance is inferred from actual behavior rather than from ratings or preference rankings. Research analysts who prefer measures based on respondent behavior may find this a technique they can apply to good advantage for some situations.

Computer Content Analysis (Semiotics)

In comparison with all other hot-button techniques, computer content analysis could be considered "far out." It is based on computer storing and analysis of comments offered by participants in focus groups or one-on-one depth interviews on a specific topic or product and/or service category. In all of these venues, respondent comments are carefully recorded by audio- or videotape. *Every spoken word* from each respondent is then entered into computer memory. (Quester[1] now has more than 1 billion words in its data warehouse computer.) Then, the following processing sequence takes place for each venue that is devoted to a specified topic (in this case, customer satisfaction):

1. Convert all words into ideas (e.g., "self" = I, me, myself, self; "want responding" = want, wanted, need, needs).

---

[1]Communication Development Company, West Des Moines, Iowa.

2. Count frequency of each idea (f); divide by total number of words spoken (f/T) to obtain percentage Observed Occurrence (%O). Subtract Expected Occurrence (%E) (from Quester database); divide by amount of variance (s.d.) in usage of this idea across organizations in the American society:

$$\frac{\%O - \%E}{s.d.} = t \text{ ratio.}$$

High t values show which ideas are operating for each respondent.

3. Determine meaning of ideas or word groups (e.g., "spring" could mean water out of the ground, a season, a coil, or a leap; "star" could mean celestial body or celebrity). For potentially ambiguous words, computer scans or calculates up to 100 words on each side and uses these words to categorize each idea properly ("computer disambiguation"). Human analyst checks (usually finds only 1% error) to provide context in which word occurs (pragmatics). This process is called *Key Words in Context*. These key words/word groups/ideas are, of course, likely to be the "hot buttons" for which we are looking.

4. Human analyst performs "Aristotelian" analysis of each key word, including definition, explanation, and implication. Implications suggest actions clients should take. The real objective is to understand what people *mean* by what they say (i.e., "deep structure" of sentences) or what meaning they take away from an advertising message.

Here is an example of this sequence:

In the late 1970s, many U.S. banks said the following in their advertisements: "We've got good news for customers. A major change in federal regulations allows us to pay *interest* directly on checking accounts."

However, the word "pay" means the following to customers: "You can *pay* your bills," "Don't have to run around to *pay* bills," or "Easy way to *pay* bills."

Therefore, customers interpreted the advertisement to mean: "I will have to *pay* money out of my pocket," or "I will have to *pay* interest on my checking account."

The advertisement should be rewritten to read:
"You will now be able to *earn interest* on the money in your checking account."

Another example is shown in Figure 5.1, which depicts the opening statement of a lawyer representing a large corporation in litigation involving a contraceptive product. In this case, Quester analysis demonstrated several rather negative connotations for the words "corporation" and "marketing." Analysts suggested that these should be replaced by "company" and "selling," which have much more positive associations.

▼ **FIGURE 5.1 QUESTER ANALYSIS OF LAWYER'S OPENING STATEMENT**

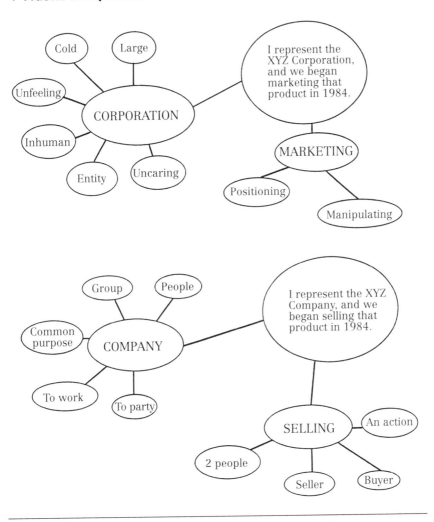

Source: Communication Development Company, West Des Moines, Iowa.

Advantages

- • • Key words indicate attributes and issues of greatest importance to respondents (the hot buttons);
- • • It reveals real, deep structure meanings on the basis of respondents' own spoken words about topic; and
- • • For direct service encounters (e.g., with bank tellers), it enables researchers to compare customers' "scripts" (how they use words) with those of service provider personnel.

Disadvantages

- • • Some cost is involved for skilled interviewers and computer content analysis,
- • • It may lack empirical validation in a specific application, and
- • • It is based on the assumption that the most important attributes and ideas are those mentioned most often.

Computer content analysis based on semiotics is probably most useful in higher profile situations that involve campaign politics, public policy issues, corporate litigation, and product/brand positioning. All of these contexts involve major issues that can be resolved only by an intensive understanding of the exact meaning of words and phrases *to people*, not based on dictionary definitions. However, computer semiotics also could be useful for uncovering the hot buttons in a customer satisfaction program within a large company, where much is also at stake.

Strategic Cube Analysis

In their challenging book *The Marketing Revolution*, Clancy and Shulman (1991) point out limitations of several popular techniques for identifying important attributes and benefits that are likely to be candidates for an effective positioning strategy. Then, they present an approach they call "Strategic Cube Analysis," which they believe is much more useful than quadrant analysis and other widely used techniques:

> A Strategic Cube Analysis begins with ... [an] ... audit of tangible and intangible attributes and benefits.... The more the greater; the company wants an exhaustive list that goes far beyond the me-too strategies that generally fill the marketplace. Ideally, the list includes creative, thought-provoking, innovative attributes and benefits—things like "a motor tuned to a throaty growl," "short-throw manual shift," "four-wheel double-wishbone

suspension," "razor-sharp handling," and "no-deductible, 'bumper-to-bumper' warranty".

Strategic Cube Analysis estimates the motivating power of each of approximately 75 to 100 rational and emotional attributes. It identifies the ones that are

• • • highly motivating,
• • • credible, and
• • • preemptible versus the competition.

Clancy and Shulman believe that one advantage of their technique is that it "doesn't overstate the importance of generic and rational features." This gives intangible attributes a better chance to emerge as strong positioning candidates.

The first step is to illustrate each attribute and benefit with a visual stimulus—typically a photograph. Then, each respondent is asked to indicate how desirable the attribute is to them, using a 9-point scale (9 = Extremely desirable, 1 = Extremely undesirable). In contrast to most conventional market research, this enables respondents to indicate attributes that might be "negatively motivating"—those that really turn them off. They believe that the word "importance," along with a verbal description only, leads people to give the most rational responses. However, "desirability" is a less loaded word that, with a visual show of the attribute, allows people to respond more freely. This is the *affective* component of the technique.

The next step is to ask respondents to rate the performance of both the company's and the competitors' product and/or service on the same attributes and benefits, using a 5-point scale (5 = Describes completely, 1 = Does not describe at all). Then the gap between these performance ratings and the desirability ratings obtained previously shows what each respondent believes about the ability of each competitor to deliver what is wanted. This is the *cognitive* component of Strategic Cube Analysis.

Then they "attempt to go beyond people's reports of what they want by probing beneath the surface to discover what they really want, an analysis done by correlating brand and image characteristics with actual behavior for each respondent—the *behavioral* component" (Clancy and Shulman 1991, p. 112).

Next, the computer weights each of these 3 measures to arrive at an overall measure of the motivating power for each attribute and benefit for each respondent. Then, a strategic cube is constructed for each respondent, as indicated in Figure 5.2 for a hypothetical respondent named George T. Jones.

▼ FIGURE 5.2 STRATEGIC CUBE ANALYSIS

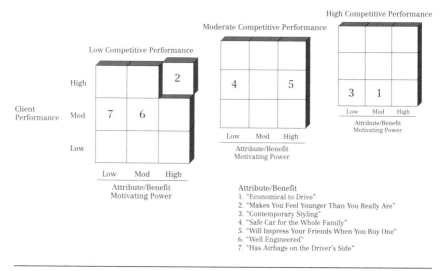

Source: Clancy, Kevin J. and Robert S. Shulman (1991), *The Marketing Revolution: A Radical Manifesto for Dominating the Marketplace*. New York: Harper Business.

This example shows that 7 attributes have the greatest motivating power for George. Benefit 2

> captures Ponce de Leon effect; it promises to 'make you feel younger than you really are.' For 57-year-old George, this is 'high' in motivating power, 'high' in perception of client performance, and 'low' in perceptions of competitive performance.... Attributes and benefits that are high in motivating power and where the company's product enjoys an edge over the competition represent wonderful opportunities for positioning and for message strategies (Clancy and Shulman 1991, p. 113).

Advantages

- • • It integrates 3 separate measures of importance to arrive at a single measure of "motivating power,"
- • • It enables researchers to consider the strength of the client company in relation to the competition, and
- • • It does this at the individual respondent level.

Disadvantages

- • • It requires many ratings for each respondent,
- • • It is analysis intensive, and

• • • No information about weights is used to produce a "motivating power" index.

CHOOSING AMONG METHODS

With so many methods, both direct and indirect, from which to choose, how do we decide among them? Is there a single "best" method for all applications and types of studies? Unfortunately, no. The choice depends on several factors, including study objectives, number of attributes, types of attributes, and the philosophical leanings of the researcher and his or her management. Some people feel more comfortable with direct methods, others with indirect. This will always be the case. Unfortunately, as was noted previously, direct and indirect methods often give quite different results for some attributes. This poses a dilemma that cannot be resolved easily. The purpose here has been simply to point out that several methods exist and describe briefly the most useful of these in the typical customer satisfaction research context.

However, one solution to this dilemma is to use *both direct and indirect methods* in the same study when this is feasible. Perhaps the simplest way to do this is to ask respondents for both importance *and* performance ratings for all attributes. Then researchers can obtain both mean importance ratings (direct measure) and correlations of performance ratings with some overall satisfaction or likelihood of switching measure (indirect measure) for each attribute. These two measures can be plotted, with the indirect measure on the vertical axis and the direct measure on the horizontal axis for each attribute. An example of this is shown in Figure 5.3 for a study of factors and features that drive perceptions of automobile quality, conducted by the J.D. Power and Associates.

Note the great amount of disagreement between direct and indirect results for most car quality attributes. If both methods were in agreement, the pattern of dots would lie on or close to a diagonal line from the lower left- to upper right-hand corners of the plot. Clearly they do not, and this is very typical. Some features are completely divergent. For example, both "oil gauge" and "oil dipstick maintenance" are rated among the highest in importance, yet they both show the lowest correlations with overall car quality ratings. How do we reconcile or use these divergent findings?

Cost of Entry

One way to address divergent findings is to use the plot to identify specific attributes that *must* be present in a product and/or service

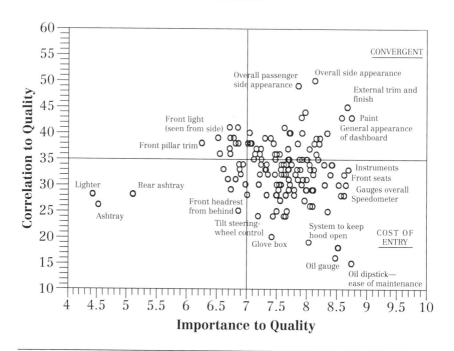

Source: J.D. Power and Associates.

but that offer no special advantage, often because every competitor has them. I call these "cost of entry" attributes. They can be identified using both direct and indirect measures of attributes together.

Cost of entry attributes would be those in the lower right-hand quadrant of the plot. Respondents *say* they are important, but they do not drive overall satisfaction to any great extent, based on correlation analysis. However, because people think and say these attributes are important, they probably should be an integral part of any competitive product and/or service offering. They are the ante a company must pay to play in the poker game of the marketplace. A company might not want to commit large resources to improving these because they do not drive overall satisfaction much. However, it should proceed with caution before de-emphasizing or eliminating any of these features or attributes. They might be very important to customers. At least respondents think they are.

Of course, the best attributes on which to focus company resources are the ones in the upper right-hand quadrant. These might be called "convergent" items. People say they are important, and they also correlate highly with some overall satisfaction measure. Either way, these attributes are almost certainly most important to respondents. There are usually a rather small number of them, as opposed to the very large numbers of attributes people *rate* high in importance, and this makes it a great deal easier for a company to know on what to concentrate its resources.

Best Single Approach

When only a single importance measure can be used, many experienced survey researchers tend to prefer one of the indirect methods, because these show attributes that are most likely to drive or affect overall satisfaction. If the task involves only a few objective product and/or service *features*, the usual preference is for one of the forms of conjoint analysis. If only 5 to 8 features are to be considered, full-profile conjoint tends to be used. When more features are involved, the Sawtooth version of pairwise trade-off conjoint often is preferred. Any of these usually provide a reasonably accurate measure of attribute importance for each individual respondent and for a total sample.

In contrast, when large numbers of attributes are rated on a continuous scale, it is usually best to use correlation/regression analysis in one of the ways discussed previously in Chapter 4. (Again, we must be careful to avoid highly collinear attributes when using multiple regression analysis.) Regression analysis usually can be performed only at the aggregate level, with rather large numbers of respondents. However, because most markets are not homogeneous in terms of attribute importance, it is sometimes better first to segment the market in some meaningful way in terms of overall preferences or behavior and then perform correlation/regression analysis within each segment, as well as across the total market. Or, the method of extreme differences could be used to obtain attribute importances for each individual respondent.

REFERENCES

Clancy, Kevin J. and Robert S. Shulman (1991), *The Marketing Revolution: A Radical Manifesto for Dominating the Marketplace*. New York: Harper Business.

Jaccard, James, David Brinberg, and Lee J. Ackerman (1986), "Assessing Attribute Importance: A Comparison of Six Methods," *Journal of Consumer Research*, 12 (March), 463–68.

Lehmann, Donald R. and William L. Moore (1980), "Validity of Information Display Boards: An Assessment Using Longitudinal Data," *Journal of Marketing Research*, 17 (November), 450–59.

CHAPTER 6

COMPARISONS AMONG METHODS

The previous 3 chapters present approximately a dozen different methods for determining the relative importance of product and/or service attributes. It was repeatedly pointed out that different methods often produce different results, even within a major type (e.g., direct, indirect). In this chapter, we

• • • Demonstrate these differences by presenting comparisons of the results obtained from using different methods in the same study with the same respondents;

• • • Compare results from stated (rated) importance versus correlated importance for the same respondents in a wide variety of product and/or service categories studied;

• • • Suggest ways of reducing overlap among similar attributes, using factor analysis, correlation analysis, and judgment; and

• • • Show how to consolidate both importance and performance measures into a single graphic plot (a Quadrant Analysis) for maximum impact and understanding.

A central theme of the previous chapters has been that one reason a variety of approaches to measuring attribute importance has been developed is because different methods can produce different results or outcomes. One good example of this problem is Chapter 3's comparison of stated versus correlated importance of attributes for a large utility company in the United States (Table 3.1). In that study, there was little agreement between these 2 methods. This can be a real problem when deciding on the attributes to be rated in an ongoing customer satisfaction study, as well as on where to concentrate improvement efforts. As was suggested previously, a pretest should be performed to identify the best attributes to rate. However, if different methods produce different results, how do we know which method(s) to believe?

COMPARISONS AMONG 6 METHODS

Probably the most comprehensive comparative study ever performed was by Jaccard, Brinberg, and Ackerman (1986), who compare 6 different approaches to measuring attribute importance:

1. Elicitation,
2. Subjective probabilities,
3. Information display board frequency,
4. Information display board order,
5. Direct ratings, and
6. Conjoint analysis (full profile).

These methods were compared across 9 common attributes in each of 2 product categories: cars and birth-control methods. (Attributes were different for the 2 categories, of course.) A single group of college-student respondents was asked to perform the required tasks for each of the 6 methods in each of the 2 product categories. Analyses were carried out by the authors, as prescribed by each method. Tables 6.1 and 6.2 show results for cars and birth-control methods, respectively. Entries in the tables are correlation coefficients of attribute importance measures between pairs of methods, pooled across all 9 attributes (only 4 for conjoint) and all respondents. Coefficients below the diagonal are from cross-individual analysis (i.e., correlating the 2 importance values for each pair of methods across all respondents); those above the diagonal are from aggregate-level analysis (pooling all respondents before conducting the importance comparisons for each pair). Correlation coefficients can range from .00 to ±1.00; +1.00 indicates a perfect relationship, which is almost never found in working with real data, except when using rank-order correlations.

▼ TABLE 6.1 AVERAGE CORRELATION AMONG IMPORTANCE INDICES: CARS

Methods	E	SP	IDBF	IDBO	DR	CJ
Elicitation (E)	—	.19	.15	.22	.19	.28
Subjective probability (SP)	.08	—	.28	.25	.62	.68
Information display board frequency (IDBF)	.12	.12	—	.78	.22	.19
Information display board order (IDBO)	.14	.11	.49	—	.25	.15
Direct rating (DR)	.13	.37	.09	.13	—	.58
Conjoint analysis (CJ)	.09	.11	.10	.11	.11	—

Note: Average correlation with conjoint measures is based on 4 attributes; others are based on 9. Lower off-diagonal elements are from across-individual analysis. Upper off-diagonal elements are from aggregate-level analysis.

Source: Jaccard, James, David Brinberg, and Lee J. Ackerman (1986), "Assessing Attribute Importance: A Comparison of Six Methods," *Journal of Consumer Research*, 12 (March), 463–68. Used with permission from the University of Chicago.

▼ TABLE 6.2 AVERAGE CORRELATION AMONG IMPORTANCE INDICES: BIRTH-CONTROL

Methods	E	SP	IDBF	IDBO	DR	CJ
Elicitation (E)	—	.30	.15	.19	.33	.23
Subjective probability (SP)	.08	—	.15	.15	.66	.33
Information display board frequency (IDBF)	.12	.11	—	.82	.19	.19
Information display board order (IDBO)	.10	.13	.49	—	.58	.15
Direct rating (DR)	.07	.38	.11	.09	—	.22
Conjoint analysis (CJ)	.11	.10	.12	.09	.10	—

Note: Average correlation with conjoint measures is based on 4 attributes; others are based on 9. Lower off-diagonal elements are from across-individual analysis. Upper off-diagonal elements are from aggregate-level analysis.

Source: Jaccard, James, David Brinberg, and Lee J. Ackerman (1986), "Assessing Attribute Importance: A Comparison of Six Methods," *Journal of Consumer Research*, 12 (March), 463–68. Used with permission from the University of Chicago.

For the most part, results for the 2 product categories (cars and birth-control methods) are surprisingly similar, considering the vast differences in their characteristics. Most cross-individual correlations (below the diagonal) are approximately .10, ± .03, for both categories. Squaring these values (r^2) gives us the percentage of overlap, or the percentage with which any 2 methods agree in their measures of attribute importance—it is only 1%-2%, maximum! The 2 exceptions for the car category are subjective probabilities and direct ratings ($r = .37$, $r^2 = 14\%$) and both information display board (IDB) measures ($r = .49$, $r^2 = 24\%$), neither of which show agreement high enough for any real confidence. Results for birth-control measures are almost identical for these two pairs of methods.

Results at the aggregate level are more encouraging, with coefficients for birth-control methods at .82 for the information display board methods, .66 for subjective probabilities versus direct ratings, and .58 for direct ratings versus information display board order. Other than these, however, there are none in excess of .33, and many are less than .20. Similarly, results for cars show only 4 coefficients in excess of .28, and 2 of these were also high for birth-control methods.

Thus, though some pairs of methods show somewhat similar results at the aggregate level (in terms of the rank order of attribute importance), most pairs do not do so at a level that gives us any confidence that we are getting the same measures of importance, regardless of what methods we use. Jaccard, Brinberg, and Ackerman (1986, p. 466) conclude:

> The present results suggest that the conclusion made about attribute importance may be quite different depending on the method used to assess importance. Clearly, further research is needed on what the different indices are in fact measuring.... Alternatively, one could conceptualize importance as a multidimensional concept in which each of the measures taps into different aspects of importance.... A multidimensional approach would require an elaboration of the conceptual foundations of the dimensions underlying attribute importance and how these map onto product evaluation.

It is this writer's personal belief that importance will ultimately be regarded as a multidimensional construct, as these authors suggest. This would mean that the term "importance" would eventually be discarded in favor of terms such as:

• • • Self-explicated importance (i.e., what I think I believe, or should believe, about each attribute of this product and/or service category),

• • • Intention importance (how attributes drive intention to purchase),

• • • Behavioral importance (similar, but for actual purchase or disloyalty),

- • Satisfaction importance (how attributes drive after-purchase product and/or service customer satisfaction),
- • and the like.

If true, this means that the concept of importance will probably never be measured adequately by any single method. The method(s) selected will depend on the objectives, the type(s) of importance of interest, and the meaning of the term "importance."

COMPARISONS FOR FOOD BLENDERS

In another study, Heeler, Okechuku, and Reid (1979) compare 3 importance methods in a study of food blenders:

- • Conjoint analysis (full profile),
- • Information display board frequency, and
- • Constant sum.

The same subjects evaluated several models of blenders on 10 attributes/features using all 3 methods. Because all of these produce importance weights for each respondent, it was possible to correlate these weights between each pair of methods separately, pooled across all attributes and respondents. Results are shown in Table 6.3.

The highest correlation was approximately .60, between conjoint analysis and constant sum methods, which indicates an agreement of approximately 35%. With a sample of approximately 100, this was statistically significant at the 95% confidence level, not high but meaningful. The next highest correlation was .53 (r^2 = 28%), between constant sum and the display board, significant at only the 90% confidence lev-

▼TABLE 6.3 INTERCORRELATIONS AMONG 3 IMPORTANCE MEASURES FOR FOOD BLENDERS

Methods	CJ	IDBF	CS
Conjoint full profile (CJ)			
Information display board frequency (IDBF)	.32[c]	—	—
Constant sum (CS)	.59[a]	.53[b]	—

[a]Significant at $p < .05$.
[b]Significant at $p < .10$.
[c]Not significant.
Source: Heeler, Roger M., Chike Okechuku, and Stan Reid (1979), "Attribute Importance: Contrasting Measurements," *Journal of Marketing Research*, 16 (February), 60–63.

el. The remaining correlation between conjoint and the display board was .32 ($r^2 = 10\%$), which was not statistically significant. Overall, these results showed some meaningful relationships among the different methods, but they also produced results that are *more different than similar*. Heeler, Okechuku, and Reid (1979, p. 62) conclude:

> Overall the lack of commonality among the three measures arising from different branches of marketing research makes plain the need for contrasting different conceptualizations (of attribute importance) and their resulting measures in marketing.

Myers and Alpert (1977) observe a great deal of semantic confusion among 3 terms in attribute importance research: salience, importance, and determinance. They note that these terms are often confused and are sometimes used interchangeably. Heeler, Okechuku, and Reid (1979, p. 62) suggest that "perhaps self-report is a measure of salience, conjoint a measure of importance, and IDB, by being the closest facsimile to actual shopping, obtains the determinant attributes." Obviously, there is no clear convergence among these measurement methods or definitions.

COMPARISONS FOR CONSUMER PRODUCT CONCEPTS

A very large comparative study was conducted by Griffin and Hauser (1993) using "consumer product concepts" that were not specified. They asked 1400 respondents to review 7 new product concepts in terms of how well the concepts would satisfy their needs. They were also given a list of 198 possible needs to refer to in making these evaluations. They were first asked to select a few needs for each "priority group" (e.g., primary needs, secondary needs). They were then asked to indicate how important each of those needs was to them, using 3 methods:

1. Direct rating (9-point scale),
2. Constant sum for each priority group separately (100 points), and
3. Anchored scale (10 points for most important need within each priority group, up to 10 points for each secondary need within each priority).

Results are shown in Table 6.4 in terms of *rank order correlations* between importance values from pairs of methods, pooled across all respondents.

For each respondent's self-designated primary needs (consisting of their top 6–7 attributes), correlations were extremely high, from .96

▼ TABLE 6.4 INTERCORRELATIONS AMONG 3 IMPORTANCE MEASURES (CONSUMER PRODUCT CONCEPTS) (N = 1400)

Methods	Direct	Anchored
Primary Needs		
Anchored	.96	—
Constant sum	.96	1.00
Secondary Needs		
Anchored	.78	—
Constant sum	.67	.94
Tertiary Needs		
Anchored	.84	—
Constant sum	.71	.89

Source: Griffin, Abbie and John R. Hauser (1993), "The Voice of the Customer," *Marketing Science*, 12 (Winter), 1-26.

to 1.00. For secondary needs, correlations ranged from .67 to .94, and for tertiary needs, they ranged from .71 to .89. These results are much more encouraging than those in the previous study, especially for attributes that are considered primary needs. One of the reasons for this is that correlations were in terms of *rank orders of attribute importance* rather than actual importance values produced by each of the 3 methods. In such a context, rank order correlations are almost always much higher. Also, 2 of the methods were similar (direct versus anchored ratings). Nevertheless, results here are far more encouraging than for the previous comparisons.

Griffin and Hauser (1993) also test the hypothesis that consumers will mention (i.e., by elicitation) those needs (attributes) they believe are most important. For each need, they compare the number of times it was mentioned with its direct ratings of importance on the 9-point scale. They find that "important needs (based on ratings) are no more likely to be mentioned by a consumer than needs in general" (p. 19) for a portable food-carrying device. They conclude that "frequency of mention does not appear to be a good surrogate for importance" (p. 19). These 2 direct methods of measuring importance (ratings and elicitation) produced very different results in this study.

Griffin and Hauser also find that direct, anchored, and constant sum ratings had "very high" correlations with both interest in and preference for the 7 concepts, but correlated importance did not (r = -.36 with interest and -.14 with preference). (These results are surprising, because importance correlations were presumably with measures of interest and preference.)

COMPARISONS OF RATED AND CORRELATED IMPORTANCE

The remainder of this chapter presents comparisons of results from only 2 methods: (1) stated importance (direct method) from ratings on 5- to 10-point scales and (2) correlated importance (indirect method) from computing correlation coefficients between attribute *performance* ratings and ratings of overall satisfaction or usage frequency, pooled across all survey respondents. These are among the most widely used methods and the most feasible for customer satisfaction studies. Correlated importance can be calculated either one attribute at a time (simple regression) or with all attributes combined (multiple regression). Most of the following studies are based on simple pairwise correlations (to avoid the problem of collinearity in interpreting beta coefficients in multiple regression models).

Nearly all of these comparisons were made using large samples of a cross section of appropriate respondents (not business students). Comparisons are based on the same respondents' ratings of the same attributes in a single survey. Data of this kind are often available or can be easily obtained. This is in line with the recommendation at the end of Chapter 5 that, whenever possible, attribute importance should be measured in at least 2 ways (direct and indirect) in a single study for a more complete picture of the factors that drive customer satisfaction.

Amusement Park

A study of a large amusement park on the West Coast produced the results shown in Figure 6.1. Open bars represent stated importance, in terms of the percentage of respondents checking the top box on a 10-point importance rating scale. Shaded bars represent correlated importance, in terms of squared correlation coefficients, showing the percentage of the overall satisfaction rating that is explained, or accounted for, by each attribute separately. Although the 2 scales represent very different constructs, a similar metric affords an opportunity for easy comparisons of these measures of attribute importance. What we are looking for is a similar *pattern* of relative importances for the 2 measures.

In this study, we find high agreement between stated and correlated importance for many attributes: "whole family enjoys together," "place my children love," "good value for money," and several others. These are the "sure things"—people say they are important, and correlations confirm this. In contrast, there are wide differences for "lines

▼ FIGURE 6.1 CORRELATED VERSUS STATED IMPORTANCE OF ATTRIBUTES (AMUSEMENT PARK)

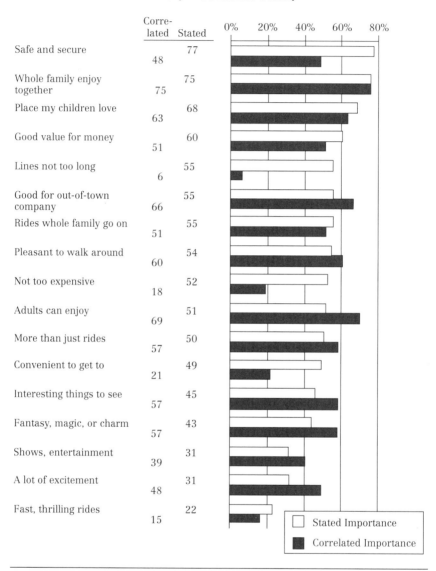

	Correlated	Stated
Safe and secure	48	77
Whole family enjoy together	75	75
Place my children love	63	68
Good value for money	51	60
Lines not too long	6	55
Good for out-of-town company	66	55
Rides whole family go on	51	55
Pleasant to walk around	60	54
Not too expensive	18	52
Adults can enjoy	69	51
More than just rides	57	50
Convenient to get to	21	49
Interesting things to see	57	45
Fantasy, magic, or charm	57	43
Shows, entertainment	39	31
A lot of excitement	48	31
Fast, thrilling rides	15	22

□ Stated Importance
■ Correlated Importance

not too long," "not too expensive," "convenient to get to," and some others. People tend to overstate the importance of safety and security (this is often found) and understate the importance of adult enjoyment, which has the second highest correlation with overall satisfaction.

Which of these 2 measures is the most accurate? As I indicated previously, I prefer correlated importance, but others may feel differently.

Casino Resort

Figure 6.2 presents results from similar analyses of ratings of a particular casino resort in Las Vegas. Again, we find agreement for some attributes but disagreement for many others, including "comfortable atmosphere," "glamorous, exciting place," and "unique/different rooms." In every case, correlated importance suggests (but does not prove, of course) that people may be underestimating the impact of these factors, as well as a few others. Most of these might be characterized as "warm, fuzzy feeling" types of attributes, and other research in public opinion polling has shown that people often underestimate or understate factors of this kind.

Children's Cars

Figure 6.3 shows results from a study of $2–$3 cars with which small children play (parents gave these ratings). Again, there is good agreement for some attributes (e.g., good value, durable), but here we find more disagreement between stated and correlated importance than in the previous studies. Notice especially the "brand I trust" attribute, which shows the highest correlated importance but only a modest stated importance. The same pattern is evident for "attractive-looking," "new models," "wide variety," "bright colors," and so forth. Conversely, safety and fun demonstrate much higher stated than correlated importance, as is often the case.

Other Studies

Several additional studies have been performed over a long period of time and in many product and/or service categories. Results are too voluminous to be shown here in bar chart form. Instead, comparisons are presented in terms of correlation coefficients between the importance values calculated by correlations and those from average rated importance, across all attributes within each study. These correlations are presented in terms of r^2 values, which show (roughly) the percentage overlap between the 2 sets of values (with a theoretical maximum of 100%).

Table 6.5 shows 12 studies with r^2 values that range from a high of 60% to a low of less than 1%. The 3 comparisons presented in the preceding bar charts are listed first. The 60% overlap for convenience

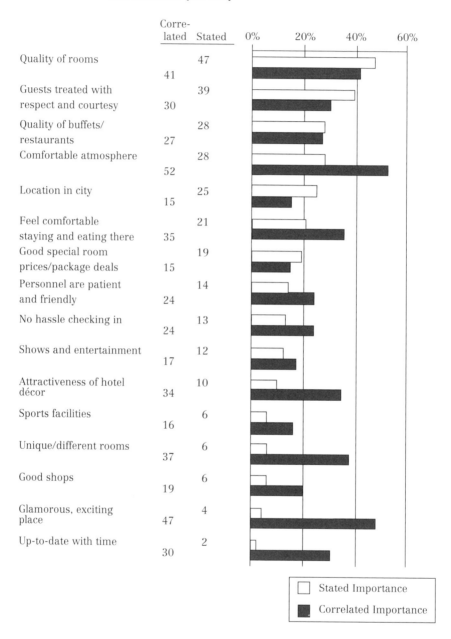

▼ FIGURE 6.2 CORRELATED VERSUS STATED IMPORTANCE OF ATTRIBUTES (HOTEL)

	Corre-lated	Stated
Quality of rooms		47
	41	
Guests treated with respect and courtesy		39
	30	
Quality of buffets/restaurants		28
	27	
Comfortable atmosphere		28
	52	
Location in city		25
	15	
Feel comfortable staying and eating there		21
	35	
Good special room prices/package deals		19
	15	
Personnel are patient and friendly		14
	24	
No hassle checking in		13
	24	
Shows and entertainment		12
	17	
Attractiveness of hotel décor		10
	34	
Sports facilities		6
	16	
Unique/different rooms		6
	37	
Good shops		6
	19	
Glamorous, exciting place		4
	47	
Up-to-date with time		2
	30	

☐ Stated Importance
■ Correlated Importance

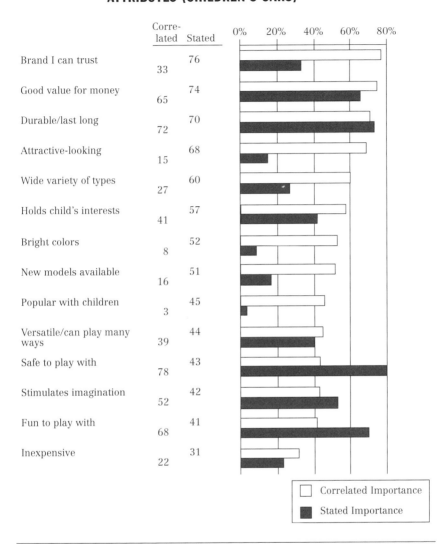

	Corre-lated	Stated
Brand I can trust	33	76
Good value for money	65	74
Durable/last long	72	70
Attractive-looking	15	68
Wide variety of types	27	60
Holds child's interests	41	57
Bright colors	8	52
New models available	16	51
Popular with children	3	45
Versatile/can play many ways	39	44
Safe to play with	78	43
Stimulates imagination	52	42
Fun to play with	68	41
Inexpensive	22	31

☐ Correlated Importance
■ Stated Importance

stores shows more agreement than disagreement but still has nowhere near perfect congruence. All of the rest show more dis-agreement than agreement, and several have overlaps of only 10% or less (photographic equipment, snack foods, and airlines). There are too few categories here to be able to generalize as to the types of prod-ucts and/or services for which agreement is more or less likely to be

TABLE 6.5 CORRELATIONS BETWEEN STATED AND INFERRED IMPORTANCE

	r^2
Amusement park (17 attributes)	16%
Casino resort (16 attributes)	4
Children's cars (14 attributes)	1
Airlines (21 attributes)	*
Snack foods (14 attributes)	10
Subcompact cars (11 attributes)	2
Dry cat food (99 attributes)	46
Soft, moist cat food (99 attributes)	41
Credit processing systems (64 attributes)	34
Convenience stores (60 attributes)	60
Seafood (74 attributes)	18
Photographic equipment (290 attributes)	10

*Less than 1%.

found. A study by Hughes and Guerrero (1971) finds "large differences" between stated and correlated importance.

CONCLUSION

All of the preceding suggest the following conclusions, relative to methods for determining the "importance" of attributes used to measure customer satisfaction:

• • • The measured importance of product and/or service attributes will often vary, depending on the method employed.
• • • This is true even within a general type of approach (e.g., direct versus indirect), and is probably even more true between the 2 major types of approaches.
• • • This clearly suggests the need for measuring importance in more than one way, at least with one direct and one indirect method, and then plotting the results from each method to get attributes that are high on both measures.
• • • The divergence of results strongly suggests that "importance" is not a unidimensional construct, that there are different types of importance, as was mentioned previously, and that each type should have its own label for the sake of clarity.

Perhaps additional research will provide a more definitive answer to the question of how best to identify the key attributes to be included in customer satisfaction surveys. Until then, I recommend the use of at least one indirect method (correlations or conjoint analysis) in addition to one or more direct methods (importance ratings or constant sum). This matter is too important to be left to a priori managerial judgment, especially when the compensation of company employees is involved, as is often the case. Customer satisfaction measurement is not an exact science, but it can be performed with greater accuracy than it is in many companies today.

ELIMINATING REDUNDANCY

All of the prior discussion and analysis have focused on the relative importance of attributes, so that only the most important ones are included in a customer satisfaction questionnaire. But this is only a first step. Many of these important attributes overlap with others because they are slightly different ways of expressing the same basic idea. These overlaps must be eliminated to keep the questionnaire as short as possible. This will reduce respondent fatigue and increase the response rate. It will also reduce survey cost.

The best way to identify redundancy is with a factor analysis of all the attributes included in a pretest. Factor analysis is a statistical technique for "data reduction." The objective is to reduce a large number of related variables to a few basic, underlying ideas that capture the essence of most of the variables. These underlying ideas are called "factors," and the purpose of a factor analysis is to determine how many basic ideas there are and how best to measure them. In the case of CSM, the variables are the various attributes rated by respondents in a pretest (perhaps 50 to 100). A factor analysis will help reduce all of these attributes to a few groups (perhaps 10 to 20) of related items that represent basic aspects of company performance that are relatively unrelated to one another. Then a final set of items can be selected for rating on an ongoing basis by customers.

Therefore, data from a pretest should be analyzed in at least 3 ways:

1. *Importance analysis*, or using 2 or more of the direct and indirect approaches in Chapters 3, 4, and 5 to find the attributes that drive satisfaction;
2. *Factor analysis*, to identify overlapping items and basic underlying ideas; and
3. *Frequency distributions* of ratings, to eliminate items that do not show a meaningful dispersion of ratings (i.e., are not "sensitive").

Results from these analyses, and perhaps others, should be reviewed by research analysts first to select a tentative reduced set of attributes (perhaps 15 to 25) for inclusion in the final questionnaire. These items should then be reviewed by top management and those who will be affected by ongoing survey results, and a final set selected.

FACTOR ANALYSIS OF SUPPLIER ATTRIBUTES

The following example of a factor analysis of attributes for industrial service firms will help illustrate how such an analysis can identify item overlaps and, thus, help arrive at a reduced, final set of attributes to be rated on an ongoing basis. Not all attributes in the pretest are shown here, only a subset to illustrate the basic approach. Factors consist of groups of related attributes that tend to be *rated approximately the same* by respondents because they represent the same basic idea. The output of a factor analysis shows these groupings along with the factor loadings for each component attribute. (*Factor loadings* indicate the correlation of each item with the factor itself; the higher the loading, the better that attribute reflects the underlying meaning of the factor.)

Table 6.6 shows only the first 4 factors that emerged from an analysis of all 36 attributes in a pretest survey of approximately 200 respondents. Factor 1 comprises 8 separate attributes related to a common theme. The analysis does not tell us what this theme or basic idea is; we must infer it from the factor loadings, especially the highest loadings, which are the statements that correlate highest with the basic idea the factor represents and, therefore, are the ones that identify it best. Here, the 2 highest loadings (.86, .83) are for items that relate to drivers and delivery (good impression, treat you respectfully). These have far higher loadings than any of the others, so we might decide to name this factor "delivery capabilities," or something similar. That this is the first factor does not necessarily mean it is the most important (in the sense of driving or influencing overall satisfaction). It simply means that more of the attributes we have decided to include in the pretest relate to this basic idea than to any other.

In a similar fashion, Factor 2 is best defined by the 2 attributes with the highest loadings (both .82) (easy to understand product/rental invoices). All 4 attributes with the highest loadings deal with invoicing or billing. We might decide to name this factor "proper invoicing." The other 2 factors can be named in a similar manner.

How can we be sure these factor labels are correct? We can't. They represent our best guesses based on the factor loadings and attributes available. Why do we even need to name factors at all? In this

▼ TABLE 6.6 FACTOR ANALYSIS OF PRETEST ATTRIBUTES

Factor	Description	Loading
1	DELIVERY CAPABILITIES	
	Good impression of delivery people	.86
	Drivers treat you respectfully	.83
	Convenience of delivery schedule	.63
	Deliver product on time	.76
	Easy to understand delivery records	.51
	Representatives treat you as valued customer	.51
	Timely delivery of promotional materials	.50
	Courtesy of telephone operators	.41
2	PROPER INVOICING	
	Easy to understand product invoices	.82
	Easy to understand rental invoices	.82
	Response to billing questions	.68
	Accurate product invoices	.67
	Meet after-sales service expectations	.53
	Good value for what you pay	.51
3	SALES REPRESENTATIVE PERFORMANCE	
	Immediate access to sales representatives	.82
	Sales representatives treat you as valued customer	.73
	Responsiveness of representatives	.71
4	PRICE/VALUE	
	Good value for money	.76
	Lowest price	.69
	Schedulers treat you as valued customer	.68
	Fair sales terms/conditions	.65
	Timely delivery of literature	.59
	Cutting-edge technology	.42

case, we don't. For our pretest purposes, we are primarily interested in seeing how items group together on the basis of similar ratings so we can eliminate some of the overlapping items and thereby shorten the questionnaire. Nevertheless, when a factor analysis is completed, most companies are interested in defining the underlying "major issues" that drive satisfaction with their performance. A good factor analysis accomplishes both of these objectives at the same time, but the primary purpose in a pretest is to identify redundancy to reduce the number of statements that need to be rated by respondents on an ongoing basis.

IMPORTANCE OF SUPPLIER ATTRIBUTES

Now that we have the major issues for this industrial supplier, the next step is to determine the relative importance of each attribute. In the case of this example, only a single approach, correlation analysis, was used. Ratings on each attribute were correlated separately with the corresponding overall satisfaction ratings, pooled across all respondents. Results appear in Table 6.7, which shows both factor loadings and r^2 values. Here we find little congruence between factor loadings and the squared correlation coefficients within most factors. This is very typical. It is not surprising, because factor analysis has nothing to do with the importance of attributes in driving overall satisfaction. It simply indicates how items group together to define a factor or basic idea.

Within Factor 1, squared importance correlations (r^2) range from a high of 64% to a low of 27%. This comes as a surprise to many people because they assume that factors are relatively homogeneous (which they often are not), so they believe the attributes should correlate similarly with overall satisfaction. (Of course, this depends greatly on the lowest factor loadings—the lower the loading, the less that item defines the factor. These cut-offs are always arbitrary.) Similarly, in Factor 2, importance correlations range from a high of 66% to a low of 29%. Again, correlations with satisfaction and factor loadings show little similarity, except perhaps a slightly negative one. In contrast, Factor 3 is much more homogeneous in terms of both factor loadings and correlations, and so on. (Squared correlations add to more than 100% because of the overlap among attributes.)

PUTTING IT ALL TOGETHER

Now that we have calculated both importance and redundancy for each attribute, the next step is to use these data to help select a reduced set of items for the final questionnaire. This is the hard part, because we must consider not only all results in Table 6.7, but also frequency distributions for each item. Also, we need to decide how best to express each final item, which may involve reworking the original statements (known as "wordsmithing") to arrive at attributes that are both very clear and highly related to satisfaction. Let us see how this might work for Factor 1 in our industrial supplier example.

▼ TABLE 6.7 FACTOR ANALYSIS AND CORRELATIONS OF PRETEST ATTRIBUTES

Factor	Description	Loading	r^2
1	DELIVERY CAPABILITIES		
	Good impression of delivery people	.86	27%
	Drivers treat you respectfully	.83	40
	Convenience of delivery schedule	.63	64
	Deliver product on time	.76	60
	Easy to understand delivery records	.51	53
	Representatives treat you as valued customer	.51	64
	Timely delivery of promotional materials	.50	29
	Courtesy of telephone operators	.41	50
2	PROPER INVOICING		
	Easy to understand product invoices	.82	30
	Easy to understand rental invoices	.82	35
	Response to billing questions	.68	29
	Accurate product invoices	.67	52
	Meet after-sales service expectations	.53	44
	Good value for what you pay	.51	66
3	SALES REPRESENTATIVE PERFORMANCE		
	Immediate access to sales representatives	.82	40
	Sales representatives treat you as valued customer	.73	38
	Responsiveness of representatives	.71	49
4	PRICE/VALUE		
	Good value for money	.76	41
	Lowest price	.69	29
	Schedulers treat you as valued customer	.68	24
	Fair sales terms/conditions	.65	46
	Timely delivery of literature	.59	29
	Cutting-edge technology	.42	17

The percentages in the r^2 column are squared correlations with overall satisfaction.

Some analysts would start with the attributes with the highest factor loadings, reasoning that these best identify the basic idea represented by Factor 1. There is nothing wrong with this approach, but my preference is to start with the highest correlations within each factor,[1] because these are the items that are most likely to drive overall satisfaction. In Factor 1, 2 attributes have r^2 values of 64%. One deals with convenience of the delivery schedule, the other with representatives treating customers as "valued." Neither of these has a very high factor loading ($\geq.70$); therefore, they do not show a high degree of overlap. Assuming their frequency distributions show reasonable dispersions, we might want to select both items for the final questionnaire.

Should we select any other items in Factor 1? The next-highest r^2 value (60%) is for "deliver product on time." But this seems to be related to an item we have already decided to select, "convenience of delivery schedule." Perhaps this basic idea is already covered, and we would decide not to include the former item.

What about the first statement, "good impression of delivery people"? Even though it has the highest loading (.86), it has the lowest r^2 value with overall satisfaction (27%). We can probably do without this item, because we already have 2 attributes that reflect this factor. A similar conclusion might be reached in the case of "drivers treat you respectfully." Even though its factor loading is very high (.83), it is similar to "representatives treat you as valued customer," which we have already selected because of its much higher r^2 value (64% versus 40%). Or, we might decide to combine these 2 items as follows: "drivers/representatives treat you as a valued customer."

Any other attributes? Two have r^2 values of approximately 50% and only moderate factor loadings (indicating less overlap with the other items in this factor). We might want to include either or both of these, especially the last one, "courtesy of telephone operators," because it seems least related to other delivery aspects.

In a similar manner, we would go through the remaining factors and select 1 to 3 statements per factor, depending on the size of the factor, the loadings, r^2 percentages, and item frequency distributions. Because there was a total of 7 factors in the industrial supplier analysis, we might select 15 or so statements for the final questionnaire. These would represent the basic aspects of company performance that probably most drive satisfaction in the eyes of its customers. We must always remember that management judgment will probably add or modify our preliminary set of final items, so the total number may grow.

---

[1]That is, the raw, pairwise correlations of each attribute versus overall satisfaction.

PERFORMANCE/IMPORTANCE ANALYSIS

After the final set of attributes has been selected, they will be rated by samples of customers and, perhaps, others on an ongoing basis. Many companies present results of these ratings by combining both importance and performance for each attribute into a single plot. Such a plot can be constructed regardless of the importance measures or performance scale used. Plots of this type are referred to as Importance/Performance Analysis (also known as Quadrant Analysis). The plot in Figure 6.4 is for the same industrial supplier discussed previously.

In this plot, only a few key attributes have been entered, at the request of management (one "marker" attribute from each of several factors). Solid circles represent the latest company ratings, and open circles show comparable ratings from one year earlier to help identify progress or deterioration. Stars represent the competitor that is "best-in-class" for all major competitors on each attribute separately.

▼ **FIGURE 6.4 IMPORTANCE/SATISFACTION RELATIONSHIPS**

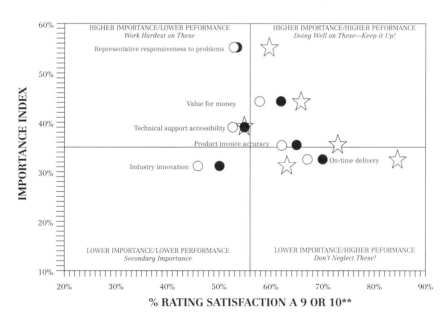

Current ratings are indicated by solid circles (●), previous ratings are indicated by open circles (○), and best-in-class are indicated by stars (☆).

For this plot, the vertical scale indicates the squared correlation (r^2) between each attribute and the overall satisfaction rating (showing the percentage these measures have in common, the correlated importance). The horizontal scale indicates the percentage of respondents rating the company a 9 or 10 on a 10-point scale, showing performance on the item. (An alternative would have been to use average or mean ratings.) The locations of horizontal and vertical dividing lines are arbitrary.

Note the prescriptions in each of the 4 quadrants that instruct the company and its employees how to interpret the plot and implement its results. Attributes in the upper right-hand quadrant are those on which the company is performing best on the most important factors (even though there is plenty of room for improvement). Employees are exhorted to "keep it up!" Those in the upper left-hand quadrant are of special interest, because the company is not doing as well on attributes that are important (especially representative responsiveness). The instruction here is to "work hardest on these" (even though the average ratings are not far below those of other attributes). Attributes in the lower left-hand quadrant are of "secondary importance." Those in the lower right-hand quadrant should not be neglected, even though their importance is lower than some others. (Unfortunately, this company tends to do better on attributes of the least importance!)

This plot shows both good and bad news. The good news is that the company has shown at least some improvement from the prior year in each of the 6 key attributes. The bad news is that 5 of the 6 attributes show performance levels lower than those of the best competitors on that attribute. A bittersweet conclusion. However, the trend is in the right direction, and the company should encourage its people to try even harder. Unfortunately, of course, the competition will probably not stand still. Other companies will almost certainly be conducting their own customer satisfaction surveys on an ongoing basis, so every company will have to work hard just to stay in place.

REFERENCES

Griffin, Abbie and John R. Hauser (1993), "The Voice of the Customer," *Marketing Science*, 12 (Winter), 1–26.

Heeler, Roger M., Chike Okechuku, and Stan Reid (1979), "Attribute Importance: Contrasting Measurements," *Journal of Marketing Research*, 16 (February), 60–63.

Hughes, G. David and Jose L. Guerrero (1971), "Testing Cognitive Models Through Computer-Controlled Experiments," *Journal of Marketing Research*, 8 (August), 291–97.

Jaccard, James, David Brinberg, and Lee J. Ackerman (1986), "Assessing Attribute Importance: A Comparison of Six Methods," *Journal of Consumer Research,* 12 (March), 463–68.

Myers, James H. and Mark I. Alpert (1977), "Semantic Confusion in Attitude Research: Salience vs. Importance vs. Determinance," in *Advances in Consumer Research*, Vol. 4, William D. Perreault Jr., ed. Atlanta, GA: Association for Consumer Research, 106–10.

CHAPTER 7

CHARACTERISTICS OF GOOD PERFORMANCE RATING SCALES

C hapter 1 presents 4 general types of rating scales that are used most often in CSM: (1) simple performance ratings, (2) simple satisfaction ratings, (3) single expectations/performance ratings, and (4) dual expectations/performance ratings. The first 2 involve ratings of company *performance* only. In this chapter, we extend the focus on performance ratings by discussing some of the basic principles of good rating-scale construction, which can help a company select a scale that is likely to be reliable, valid, and meaningful for respondents. This includes the following topics:

• • • The 4 general types of measurement scales;
• • • Types of performance rating scales, verbal versus numerical;
• • • Testing alternative scaling formats;
• • • Scale point definition semantics; and
• • • Frequency distributions and central tendency.

These topics will help companies better understand their options when constructing performance rating scales and enable them to select one or more that best fit their needs.

TYPES OF MEASUREMENT SCALES

Before discussing any other scaling matters, it is good to review some basic principles of measurement that apply to any and all types of scaling of human judgments. Good textbooks in marketing research and statistics discuss the 4 basic types of measurement scales. These apply to any measures, obtained in any way and for every type of application, not just to CSM.

- • • *Nominal* is a scale in which numbers are used for identification purposes only and no order is implied (e.g., #67 on a football jersey or a marathon runner), also referred to as "category" measurement.
- • • *Ordinal* is a scale in which numbers indicate relative value only (e.g., a rank of 1 is larger or better than 2, but no indication of how much better), usually referred to as "rank-order" scales.
- • • *Interval* is a scale in which intervals between numbers are equal everywhere on the scale,[1] but it has no 0 point (commonly found in mental testing and subjective rating/evaluation scales). These are called "interval" or "cardinal" scales.
- • • *Ratio* is a scale in which intervals between numbers are equal, and it has a 0 point (e.g., monetary amounts, age, number in family, company size in dollars or number of employees).

Companies constructing customer satisfaction measures can usually choose only between ordinal and interval scales for respondent ratings. Nominal (category) scales give no meaningful quantitative values per se, so they are not an option. At the other extreme, ratio scales cannot be used because respondent ratings are generally considered by psychometricians to have no measurable 0 point, which indicates the complete absence of the attribute in question. Thus, it is important to note that ratings by customers, even on an interval scale, *cannot be used to produce ratios*; for example, an average rating of 8 is *not* twice as high as an average rating of 4, and an average rating of 9 is *not* 50% higher than an average of 6.

---

[1]And, technically, where equal intervals on one scale are equal when mapped into an equivalent scale. For example, the difference between 55 and 45 degrees Fahrenheit (F) and between 98 and 88 F are equal. The difference between pairs of equivalent Celsius temperatures also will be equal, but not necessarily to 10 degrees. (Courtesy of Gary Mullet, Gary Mullet & Associates.)

The choice between ordinal and interval scaling for satisfaction ratings is largely a matter of personal preference. Either is acceptable, and both are in widespread use. However, it is good to keep in mind the following limitations of ordinal (rank-order) scaling:

• • • For any given respondent, the psychological distance between ranks (in terms of meaning) is unknown. For example, a rank of 2 could be nearly as good as a rank of 1, or it could be far below.
• • • Rank-order scales are "ipsative"; that is, all of the companies or salespeople being evaluated are ranked only in relation to one another and not to some external or absolute reference point. All of them might be very good, or very bad, or anywhere in between, but ranking provides no information at all about this.
• • • Ranking may be much harder than rating for respondents, especially when many companies or salespeople are being ranked.
• • • In some customer satisfaction studies, only a single company (the sponsor) or salesperson is being rated. In these circumstances, ranks are often meaningless.

Thus, most customer satisfaction studies will employ only interval scales, or scales that look like interval scales ("quasi-interval" scales). This distinction will be made clearer in the discussions that follow.

TYPES OF PERFORMANCE RATING SCALES

As was noted in Chapter 1, there are 2 generic types of scales for rating performance: (1) *verbal scales*, in which each interval on the scale has a verbal description, and (2) *numerical scales*, which are defined only by verbal anchor statements at each end. Examples of each are shown in Chapter 1 and also are provided in this chapter.

Many factors influence the choice between verbal and numerical scales for rating customer satisfaction. For example, most verbal scales contain fewer scale points than most numerical scales; the former seldom have more than 5 scale points, whereas numerical scales often have 7, 10, or more points. One reason for this is that the greater the number of intervals desired on a verbal scale, the more difficult it becomes to find words to describe each scale point, such that the psychological distances between all of the adjacent verbal labels are equal or nearly equal. Anything beyond 5 scale points on a verbal scale can be quite difficult to construct properly.

Therefore, most analysts who want a longer scale with more intervals will choose a numerical scale of some type. Many researchers believe that longer scales encourage respondents to spread their ratings across more scale points, which results in several advantages: (1)

The scale becomes more sensitive, which provides more opportunity to "move the needle" and show improvements in average ratings from one survey wave to the next; (2) A greater spread of ratings is usually better for advanced statistical analysis, such as correlations, multiple regressions (for building overall satisfaction indexes), and factor analysis; and (3) A larger number of intervals gives respondents more opportunity to discriminate and find the point on the scale with which they are most comfortable.

This latter point is particularly important when customers are rating their present suppliers, the more common situation. These ratings tend to cluster near the top of any scale, because former customers who were very dissatisfied for one reason or another have already left the company. This results in rating distributions that are highly skewed toward the lower end of the scale, as is shown in Figure 7.1. When this happens, it does not really matter how many intervals the scale has—only the top 2 or 3 are actually used by most respondents, so we have, in effect, only a 2- to 3-point scale! Adding intervals to the scale might or might not help correct this problem.

Verbal Scales

There are many types of verbal scales, some of which are shown here, in which the importance of ensuring equal psychological distances between scale points is stressed. (Figure 7.8, which appears later in this chapter, is provided to help by indicating psychological scale points for each of approximately 50 verbal descriptors that might be used.) At this point, however, let us examine more closely

▼ FIGURE 7.1 EXAMPLE OF SKEWED SCALE

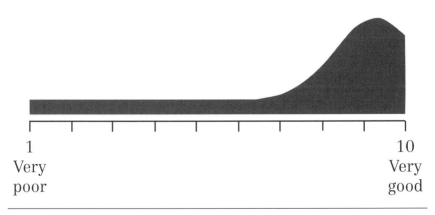

1
Very
poor

10
Very
good

one very popular verbal scale used to obtain company ratings from customers, just to see how the choice of intervals and statements might affect customer ratings.

Here is a typical, widely used 5-point verbal scale for rating a company on many satisfaction attributes:

Excellent	(70%)
Very good	(20%)
Good	(5%)
Fair	(3%)
Poor	(2%)

Assume a distribution of ratings as shown in parentheses, which could be expected for a well-run, customer-oriented company. Now suppose we eliminate the second scale point (very good), as is often done. What will happen to the distribution of ratings? Here is what we might expect:

Excellent	(80%)
(Very good)	
Good	(15%)
Fair	(3%)
Poor	(2%)

We can be rather sure that the 20% in the "Very good" box will be split between "Excellent" and "Good." To oversimplify, suppose an equal number of ratings went each way (it could be argued that more would go up than down because of the greater proportion of ratings there, but this is only conjecture). Now "Excellent" has 80% of all ratings, rather than 70%, and the company looks even better because of this. This will surely please top management, but is it as accurate a reading of customer sentiment as the original 5-point scale? Maybe not. The objective here is not to decide which is the more accurate scale but rather to demonstrate how the choice of number of intervals and verbal descriptors can greatly affect CSM results.

Likert Scaling

One very popular type of verbal scale is known as a *Likert scale*. It is a "general purpose" scale, in that it is widely used for many types of research in such areas as marketing, psychology and other behavioral sciences, and CSM. For this type of scaling, the usual approach is to phrase each attribute in the format of a statement that characterizes a person or company. For example,

• • • My bank is open when I need it.
• • • Our salesperson really understands our needs.
• • • Our supplier always responds promptly.

The respondent is asked to use the following scale for rating each attribute:

Strongly agree,
Agree,
Neither agree nor disagree,
Disagree, or
Strongly disagree.

Presumably, the psychological distances between steps are approximately equal. Many companies and research firms believe this scale is user-friendly and minimizes confusion and misunderstanding. It is also symmetrical, with the steps and labels equal above and below the neutral point. Of course, much depends on the way the statements are phrased and the strength of the adjectives and adverbs. Some companies stretch the scale by adding "Very strongly agree/disagree" at the top and bottom to make a 7-point verbal scale. This would probably work better for CSM. Thus, Likert scaling offers a verbal scale of 7 points for those who want verbal scales with more intervals than most scales offer.

Numerical Scales

By definition, the only verbal statements on most numerical scales are at either end, so they are the only ones that can influence ratings. Therefore, these terms should be selected to produce the greatest possible *dispersion* in ratings. This tends to produce greater scale sensitivity, to make it easier to move the needle from one survey wave to another. The best way to do this is with a stronger anchor at the top and a weaker one at the bottom of the scale. Using this perspective, the scale in Figure 7.2 probably does not have the best anchors to spread ratings along the scale.

▼ **FIGURE 7.2 EXAMPLE OF POORLY ANCHORED NUMERICAL SCALE**

For the top anchor, using "very" is probably not strong enough. It has an average rating of only 16–18 on the 21-point scale in Figure 7.8 (at the end of this chapter). The word "extremely," with a rating of approximately 18, would be better. Or we might use statements such as "excellent," "superior," "truly outstanding," or "completely satis-fied," all of which seem even stronger. Strong anchors of this type should help move some ratings *away* from the top boxes and toward the middle of the scale. If they even move several ratings 1 or 2 box-es lower, we will have a 4- or 5-point scale in effect, instead of a 2- or 3-point one. (With a weak top anchor, some companies that do par-ticularly well might have 70%–80% of their ratings in the top box, which, in effect, results only in a 2-point scale.)

At the other end of the scale, we need to move the bottom anchor upward so that more respondents will use the lower boxes. As it stands, the term "very bad" is so derogatory that few raters will go that low in rating companies or people with whom they currently do business. Why would customers continue to do business with suppli-ers they consider very bad on some key attributes? The solution is to strengthen the lower term to make it less derogatory. We might select such terms as "not very good," "fairly good," or "only fair." It is im-portant to note that *anchor statements need not be symmetrical.* From a psychometric perspective, the primary objective is to choose anchor statements that will produce the greatest dispersion of ratings to *maximize scale sensitivity and discrimination.*

The result of both of these anchor changes would be an improved scale, which might look like the one in Figure 7.3. This scale should produce a more disperse distribution of ratings from respondents, rather than one that is highly skewed, as in Figure 7.1. Therefore, the revised scale should be more responsive to changes in ratings from one wave to the next, making it easier to "move the needle" when im-provements are made by the company.

▼ **FIGURE 7.3 IMPROVED NUMERICAL SCALE**

How Many Intervals?

A common question asked by those who want to construct rating scales has to do with the number of intervals the scale should contain. Is there some "right number" of intervals for rating scales? (I personally have been asked this question frequently.) One study (Haley and Case 1979, p. 29) examined results from 13 different scales, both verbal and numerical, that were used for various market research purposes and concluded:

> Simply adding points to a scale in the hope of measuring finer distinctions in attitude may not work. Including more than, say, seven points may in fact lessen the power of the scale to discriminate.

Psychologists have also concluded that the maximum number of objects most people can keep in mind at one time is approximately 7. Perhaps this is the magic number for rating scale intervals. However, many companies seem comfortable with and often use 10-point scales.

Therefore, several factors should be kept in mind when deciding on an appropriate number of intervals:

- • • Verbal scales will generally have fewer intervals than numerical scales, as was mentioned previously;
- • • In general, the more intervals a scale has, the greater the possibility of ratings dispersion;
- • • More important than the number of intervals the scale contains is the number that is *used*, and this in turn depends on the choice of verbal descriptors or anchors;
- • • A careful reading of the study comparing 13 different scales reveals that, though 7-point scales were considered better, they were only slightly better than longer scales based on the criteria applied; and
- • • Ten- and 11-point scales are also in widespread use today for a variety of purposes, so respondents are very familiar with them.

What all of this suggests is that there is no single "best" number of intervals for rating scales. Perhaps a good rule of thumb would be 4 to 6 intervals for most verbal scales, and 7 to 11 intervals for most numerical scales. The decision will also depend on the preferences of top management, as well as those of the company that is being evaluated. If an outside supplier that specializes in CSM is used, its recommendations should be considered as well. Also, keep in mind that in this chapter, we are discussing only scaling that is suitable for performance ratings. In the following chapter, we consider ratings of expectations as well as performance, and this can also affect the optimum number of scale intervals.

Although there are other specialized types of rating scales (e.g., Semantic Differential, Stapel) and endless variations of all the major types of scales, the basic ideas discussed here will apply to all types of both verbal and numerical scales. Each company faces the challenge of selecting a rating scale format that is most suitable for its own characteristics and customers. If time and budget allow, it is always wise to include different types of scales in the pretest that was recommended in Chapter 1. Then, distributions of ratings can be compared to determine the best verbal descriptors or anchors to use on an ongoing basis.

TESTING ALTERNATIVE SCALING FORMATS

One company that has done extensive studies on the properties of rating scales for measuring customer satisfaction is Bellcore, the research and development arm of the Regional Bell Operating Companies in the United States and a leading provider of communications software and consulting services based on world-class research. The primary objective of one part of this work was to search for the best rating scale for its own CSM programs. Devlin, Dong, and Brown (1993) tested a wide variety of scale formats in different companies, using 6 criteria of effectiveness:

• • • Minimal response bias,
• • • Clear semantic interpretation,
• • • Discriminating power,
• • • Fits with delivery method,
• • • Ease of use by customers, and
• • • Credibleness/usefulness for supplier.

Definitions of each criteria can be found in Figure 7.4. Each of a multitude of different scales was evaluated by each of the 6 criteria, on the basis of data from surveys of different types of Bellcore customers, both business and residential. After ratings were collected from samples of respondents, Bellcore research personnel conducted personal interviews with each respondent to ascertain, on a judgmental basis, how positive or negative the respondent actually felt for each point on the scale. An example of this for one particular scale, which uses "excellent" and "terrible" as anchors, is shown in Figure 7.5.

Minimal response bias
- Minimizes positive response bias, combats the tendency to be "nice" with a politely negative or neutral category.
- Minimizes end-point avoidance, at least 2 positive and 2 negative categories avoid misinterpreting end-point avoiders.

Clear semantic interpretation
- Accounts for colloquial use of scale categories, avoids words with conflicting use, such as "fair weather" (positive), or "fair ruling" (neutral), or "only fair" (mediocre).
- Accurately reflects opinions, for example, "satisfied" reflects supplier commitment rather than customer need.
- Consistent interpretation across respondents, for example, C is an "adequate" grade to one student, but B is to another.

Discriminating power
- Distinguishes service levels, separates and defines poor versus adequate versus exceptional service.
- Avoids too many or too few rating categories:
  – sufficient gradation to drive action, and
  – only a subset is used when too many, requiring calibration and suggesting artificial gradients.
- Predicts behavior and intention, relates to likelihood to complain or recommend and purchase or repurchase.

Fit with delivery method
- Robust against or customized to delivery method, for example, in a scale presented to counterbalance positive response bias:
  – positive category stated first for interview, and
  – negative category listed first on paper.
- Introduction chosen to optimize use.
- Minimally affected by position, question order, and so forth.

Ease of use for customers
- Respondents need not "like" scale, but
  – Drop-out rate is not unusually high,
  – All categories are used,
  – Infrequent requests to *repeat* scale,
  – Consistent responses and comments, and
  – Little irritation or hesitation in interview.

Credible/useful for supplier
- Even unjustified challenges to scale redirect energy away from quality improvement; replace scale if obstacles are too great but don't let supplier dictate scale.

Source: Bellcore.

▼FIGURE 7.5 AFFECTIVE INTERPRETATION OF SCALED RESPONSES

Scaled Response	Nature of Respondent Comment		
	Positive	Mixed	Negative
Terrible, Very bad, or Bad	2	14	83
Fair	15	16	69
Good, Very good, or Excellent	70	22	8
No response	23	15	62

Source: Bellcore.

This example shows that, of all respondents who gave a rating of "terrible," "very bad," or "bad," only 2 were judged to be feeling positively toward the company, 14 had mixed feelings, and 83 were judged to feel negatively. No surprises here. But the word "fair" is much more ambiguous. A priori, it might be thought to have either slightly positive or slightly negative connotations. However, the 69 respondents who were judged to be saying something negative are a far larger group than the 15 with positive leanings, giving a rather clear indication that the word "fair" has a much more negative than positive connotation. Responses of "good," "very good," and "excellent" are generally on the positive side, as is expected, but many (22) had mixed feelings and a few (8) were on the negative side. Also, nearly 3 times as many "no responses" had negative than positive feelings!

A sample of some of the conclusions from the Bellcore research are shown in Figure 7.6 for several major types of scales that rate *performance only*. These findings deserve careful study by companies interested in selecting the best possible scale(s) for their CSM programs. Several examples are shown of low-scoring scales that fail on one or more of the criteria of effectiveness. The section concludes with 4 scales that meet or exceed most criteria and do not have serious deficiencies on any. These scales, or modifications of them, would be a good place to start for most companies.

However, it is important to keep in mind that these results came only from telephone company customers and may not apply in other

▼ **FIGURE 7.6 SCALE ASSESSMENT**

Satisfied	Dissatisfied

____ Fails to discriminate.
____ Fails to control response bias.

Excellent	Good	Fair	Poor

____ Fails semantically (meaning of "fair" ambiguous).
____ Fails to control positive response bias.
____ Poor discriminating power.

Excellent	Good	Average or Just okay	Poor	Terrible

____ Scores well on all criteria.
____ Slightly suboptimal in discriminating power.
____ Favored when expectations/requirements poorly defined.

Very satisfied	Satisfied	Somewhat dissatisfied	Very dissatisfied

____ Fails to control positive response bias.
____ Poor discriminating power.

Very satisfied	Satisfied	Somewhat satisfied	Dissatisfied	Very dissatisfied

____ Suboptimal discriminating power.

Very satisfied	Satisfied	Neither satisfied nor dissatisfied	Dissatisfied	Very dissatisfied

____ Suboptimal discriminating power.
____ Fails on telephone ("neither..." avoided).

A	B	C	D	F

____ Fails consistent semantic interpretation.

1	2	3	4	5	6	7	8	9	10

____ Fails consistent semantic interpretation.
____ Probably too many categories.
____ Potentially misleading or discriminating because of outliers/ skewness.

Much better than expected	Better than expected	Just as expected	Worse than expected	Much worse than expected

(High scoring scale)

____ Controls response bias well.

____ High discriminating power.

____ Isolates superior service.

____ Slight concern about ease of use on telephone.

____ Introduction requires defining "expectation" for semantic clarity and corporate buy-in.

____ Consistent with quality models.

Better than expected	Just as expected	Worse than expected

Similar to prior scale, but trades off easier use on telephone against reduced discriminating power and slight increase in response bias.

Standards/requirements for quality are...
Exceeded   Met   Nearly met   Missed

(High scoring scale)

____ Best control of positive response bias.

____ High discriminating power.

____ Works with all delivery methods.

____ "Exceeded" can be misused as "too long" or "too much" without careful wording.

____ Consistent with quality models/policies.

____ Strong supplier buy-in.

Outstanding   Good   Acceptable   Poor

____ Better than excellent-good-fair-poor scale.

____ Preliminary trial suggests similar to exceeded-to-missed scale.

____ May be some elevated inconsistency in using "acceptable."

____ Jury still out.

Source: Adapted from Bellcore.

situations. Also, most of them are verbal scales, which may or may not be preferred for a particular application. In that regard, note that the single numerical scale that was evaluated had *no anchor statements* at either end, whereas most numerical scales do and should. This might well have affected the outcome.

SCALE POINT DEFINITIONS

One problem that is endemic to any type of survey research is the meaning of the words used to define points on the measurement scales. Scales are not meaningful unless they are defined or "anchored" verbally in some way. This is a matter of semantics.

In the case of verbal scales especially, the objective is to select words or terms for each point on the scale so that intervals on the scale are equidistant in terms of *meaning to the respondent.* The problem is that the same word can mean different things to different people, as we saw previously in the case of the term "fair" (15 people believed it had a positive connotation, 69 a negative one) in the Bellcore studies. Although the dictionary carefully defines and illustrates words, it does not do so with the precision necessary for either the proper statistical analysis of ratings or the interpretation of survey results. What is needed is a way to measure the *psychological meaning* or *strength* of the terms used to define interval points or anchors for scales that measure customer satisfaction. Then, we have a much better idea of what respondents are telling us in their responses to survey questions involving rating scales. Two of the most feasible ways of determining semantic interpretations of verbal scale descriptions are post-survey respondent interviews and a priori psychometric scaling.

The Bellcore studies used post-survey respondent interviews. These afford an opportunity for researchers to question respondents directly after they have given their ratings and, thereby, to understand the nuances of the respondents' interpretations of rating scale points or anchors.

In contrast, a priori psychometric scaling can provide even more precise answers about semantic interpretations of possible scaling terms. In this approach, respondents are asked to give a *psychological scale value* for each verbal descriptor. In other words, they tell us what various scale point descriptors mean to them before we develop the rating scales.

One example of this approach is shown in Figure 7.7, which is taken from the Bellcore studies. A sample of respondents was asked where each of 13 evaluative terms would fall on a 10-point scale, in which 10 represents the best thing they could say about someone or some company and 0 represents the worst. It is especially interesting to note the terms at the top of the scale, where we find that "excellent" rates even higher than "completely satisfied." Apparently, being completely satisfied is not the best thing that can happen to respondents!

Another study produced psychometric scaling measures for 50 adjectives that could be used to define scale points for verbal scales or anchor the ends of numerical scales. Instructions to respondents were

▼FIGURE 7.7 SEMANTIC DIFFERENCE TEST

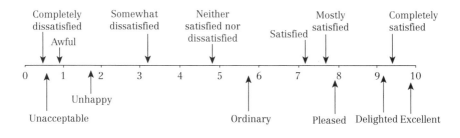

Source: Bellcore.

similar to those for the Bellcore terms in Figure 7.7, but in this case, a 21-point scale was used, and standard deviations of ratings also were calculated. The study compared results from 4 different types of respondents: homemakers, business executives, MBA students, and undergraduate business students attending a West Coast university. Each group was comprised of approximately 25–30 respondents. The results in Figure 7.8 show means and standard deviations for each word for each group of respondents.

Mean scale values reveal the psychological significance to respondents for each of the terms, that is, the degree of goodness or badness for each. Standard deviations show the dispersions, or *ranges*, of ratings and, thus, are a measure of the disagreement among respondents as to the precise scale point for each term. The greater the standard deviation, the greater the difference in interpretation among respondents is and, therefore, the greater the confusion. Note that some words have standard deviations of 3.0 or higher, which indicates that one-third of all ratings for that group were *more than ±3 scale points* from their mean ratings. Clearly, words do not have the same meanings for everyone.

These data might be helpful to readers by allowing them to select statements for a verbal scale that have approximately equal psychological distances between them at all points on the scale. The original article by Devlin, Dong, and Brown (1993) contains examples of 2 such scales that might be useful to readers who wish to construct their own customer satisfaction rating scales with care. The data also indicate the level or degree of "goodness" for each of many statements, to help understand what respondents are saying about a company, person, product, or service. Many companies give little thought to this task, apparently because they believe that one scale is as good as an-

Item	Housewives	Executives	Graduate business students	Undergraduate business students	Range of means
Superior	20.12 (1.17)	18.22 (2.82)	19.45 (1.78)	18.96 (1.67)	1.90
Fantastic	20.12 (.83)	18.69 (3.68)	20.15 (1.37)	19.20 (1.87)	1.46
Tremendous	19.84 (1.31)	18.67 (2.01)	19.70 (1.18)	18.92 (1.75)	1.17
Superb	19.80 (1.19)	19.00 (2.10)	19.40 (1.95)	19.60 (2.42)	.80
Excellent	19.40 (1.73)	18.72 (2.25)	19.58 (1.97)	19.44 (1.42)	.86
Terrific	19.00 (2.45)	18.81 (2.19)	19.08 (1.61)	18.60 (1.63)	.48
Outstanding	18.96 (1.99)	19.31 (2.01)	19.58 (1.26)	19.40 (1.35)	.62
Exceptionally good	18.56 (2.36)	17.03 (4.12)	17.68 (2.26)	17.88 (1.72)	1.53
Extremely good	18.44 (1.61)	17.33 (3.09)	17.45 (2.26)	18.00 (1.50)	1.11
Wonderful	17.32 (2.30)	17.97 (2.35)	18.45 (1.99)	17.52 (2.10)	1.13
Unusually good	17.08 (2.43)	16.47 (2.99)	16.78 (2.12)	16.20 (1.80)	.88
Remarkably good	16.68 (2.19)	17.44 (2.63)	17.20 (2.32)	17.08 (1.89)	.76
Delightful	16.92 (1.85)	16.61 (2.45)	16.60 (2.24)	16.76 (1.51)	.32
Very good	15.44 (2.77)	16.83 (2.52)	17.00 (2.18)	16.80 (1.44)	1.56
Fine	14.80 (2.12)	15.61 (2.72)	14.60 (3.00)	15.32 (2.21)	.81
Quite good	14.44 (2.76)	13.69 (2.90)	15.70 (2.08)	15.60 (1.94)	1.91
Good	14.32 (2.08)	13.81 (3.25)	14.78 (2.27)	14.56 (1.96)	.97
Moderately good	13.44 (2.23)	11.42 (2.99)	12.60 (2.55)	13.04 (1.43)	2.02
Pleasant	13.44 (2.06)	13.61 (2.43)	13.48 (2.33)	14.48 (2.14)	1.04
Reasonably good	12.92 (2.93)	11.89 (3.37)	13.85 (2.19)	14.20 (1.71)	2.31

Item	Housewives	Executives	Graduate business students	Undergraduate business students	Range of means
Nice	12.56 (2.14)	11.44 (2.79)	12.70 (2.65)	13.72 (1.77)	2.28
Fairly good	11.96 (2.42)	11.94 (3.84)	12.40 (2.24)	13.12 (2.11)	1.16
Slightly good	11.84 (2.19)	10.25 (3.14)	11.88 (2.62)	12.32 (1.52)	2.07
Acceptable	11.12 (2.59)	10.67 (3.34)	10.72 (1.96)	11.40 (2.02)	.73
Average	10.84 (1.55)	9.97 (2.34)	10.82 (1.43)	10.76 (1.05)	.87
All right	10.76 (1.42)	10.17 (3.28)	10.95 (2.15)	11.40 (1.26)	1.23
O.K.	10.28 (1.67)	10.11 (2.48)	10.58 (2.12)	11.28 (1.21)	1.17
So-so	10.08 (1.87)	8.81 (2.75)	9.52 (1.47)	10.36 (1.15)	1.55
Neutral	9.80 (1.50)	9.56 (1.90)	10.18 (2.01)	10.52 (1.16)	.96
Fair	9.52 (2.06)	9.56 (3.67)	9.20 (2.05)	10.24 (2.20)	1.04
Mediocre	9.44 (1.80)	8.11 (2.74)	8.90 (2.36)	9.36 (2.20)	1.33
Not very good	6.72 (2.82)	6.47 (2.41)	6.40 (2.05)	7.92 (2.02)	1.52
Moderately poor	6.44 (1.64)	6.83 (3.50)	6.28 (1.87)	7.24 (1.59)	.80
Reasonably poor	6.32 (2.46)	6.31 (2.19)	5.82 (1.74)	6.16 (1.57)	.50
Slightly poor	5.92 (1.96)	7.19 (2.36)	7.25 (2.00)	8.48 (1.83)	2.56
Poor	5.76 (2.09)	5.19 (2.86)	4.72 (2.51)	5.24 (1.51)	1.04
Fairly poor	5.64 (1.68)	6.67 (2.81)	6.25 (1.63)	6.72 (1.74)	1.08
Unpleasant	5.04 (2.82)	4.36 (3.02)	4.68 (2.63)	5.52 (2.06)	1.16

Item	Housewives	Executives	Graduate business students	Undergraduate business students	Range of means
Quite poor	4.80 (1.44)	4.56 (2.58)	3.62 (1.67)	4.56 (1.78)	1.18
Bad	3.88 (2.19)	3.67 (2.54)	3.85 (1.81)	4.24 (1.88)	.57
Very bad	3.20 (2.10)	2.22 (2.34)	2.70 (2.16)	3.08 (1.50)	.98
Unusually poor	3.20 (1.44)	3.08 (1.79)	3.48 (1.68)	4.16 (1.57)	1.08
Very poor	3.12 (1.17)	3.14 (2.39)	3.35 (1.99)	3.68 (1.52)	.56
Remarkably poor	2.88 (1.74)	2.75 (1.70)	3.12 (1.70)	3.92 (1.68)	1.17
Unacceptable	2.64 (2.04)	3.53 (3.42)	3.98 (2.79)	5.56 (3.06)	2.92
Exceptionally poor	2.52 (1.19)	3.19 (2.23)	3.22 (1.82)	3.52 (1.96)	1.00
Extremely poor	2.08 (1.19)	2.83 (2.14)	3.10 (1.72)	3.24 (1.76)	1.16
Awful	1.92 (1.50)	2.25 (1.46)	2.48 (1.72)	2.68 (1.86)	.76
Terrible	1.76 (.77)	2.22 (2.63)	2.05 (1.43)	1.88 (1.24)	.52
Horrible	1.48 (.87)	2.22 (2.51)	1.62 (1.15)	2.00 (1.35)	.70

Notes: In each case, the first figure is the mean, and the second (in parentheses) the standard deviation.
Source: Myers, James H. and Gregory W. Warner (1968), "Semantic Properties of Selected Evaluation Adjectives," *Journal of Marketing Research*, 5 (November), 164–68.

▼ TABLE 7.1 INTERPOINT PSYCHOLOGICAL DISTANCES FOR A COMMONLY USED EVALUATION SCALE

	Cliff	Jones and Thurstone	Myers and Warner	Vidali
Excellent		3.71	19.40	20.11
Very good	3.25	2.56	15.44	18.39
Good	2.91	1.91	14.32	16.05
Fair		.78	9.52	11.75
Poor		−1.55	5.76	6.00

	Interpoint differences			
	As used	Jones and Thurstone	Myers and Warner	Vidali
Excellent — Good	2	1.80	5.08	1.72
Very good — Fair	2	1.78	5.92	6.64
Good — Poor	2	3.46	8.56	10.05

Source: Mullet, Gary M. (1983), "Itemised Rating Scales: Ordinal or Interval?" *European Research*, (April), 49–52.

other. This is definitely not the case. The article also shows readers how to conduct a scaling study among their own customers for more current and relevant data.

Analysis of a Commonly Used Scale

There may be no verbal scale that is more often used than the following:

• • • Excellent,
• • • Very good,
• • • Good,
• • • Fair, and
• • • Poor.

In an interesting study, Mullet (1983) examined the scale properties of these commonly used terms using data from 4 different studies, as is shown in Table 7.1. Although the numbers of scale points used in these studies were not comparable, it is the psychological distance between statements *within the same scale* that is of interest. Interpoint distances for some specific scale points in each study are shown in Table 7.1.

If these were *interval* scales, all of these distances would be approximately the same within each study. Clearly, they are not. All studies show the greatest differences between "good" and "poor," and this is especially pronounced in the Vidali (1955) study. For 3 different groups of respondents (female heads of households, male heads, and teenagers of either sex), the *differences* between scale points were statistically significant at beyond the .01 level, indicating less than 1 chance in 100 that these distances are equal. (For all 3 groups combined, $p = .00000025$.) Anyone using this popular scale should be aware that it does not meet the requirements of an equal interval scale. Mullet (1983, p. 52) cautions that it is "of no higher order than ordinal" (i.e., rank order).

FREQUENCY DISTRIBUTIONS

The preceding discussion has often referred to the impact of scale length and definitions on the *frequency distributions* of respondent ratings. The usual objective of psychometricians is to construct scales that have at least a meaningful amount of dispersion (spread or range), and generally, the more dispersion the better. Greater dispersion increases scale sensitivity for analysis purposes and also gives raters more scale points to enable them to reflect their feelings more precisely. This makes it easier to reflect company improvements from one rating period to the next. However, scales in excess of 10–11 intervals are seldom found in practice. The conventional wisdom is that 10- to 11-point scales provide ample opportunity for a good range of ratings *if* they are constructed properly.

Let us look at some actual frequency distributions of ratings for one interviewing wave of a customer satisfaction survey involving approximately 20 attributes. These are performance ratings on a 10-point scale (10 = Completely satisfied, 1 = Completely dissatisfied). All of these distributions are highly skewed toward the lower end (negative skew), as would be expected from a survey of present customers only. Table 7.2, Part A shows the worst skew, with 52.7% of ratings at 10. Only 8.4% of the ratings are at or below 7, so we find only 3 scale points with frequencies greater than 10%. In contrast, Table 7.2, Part B, shows the best dispersion for this interviewing wave, with only 31.0% of the ratings at 10 and 28.1% of the ratings at 7 or lower. This gives us effectively a 5- to 6-point scale, much better than the preceding one. All of the remaining attributes were somewhere between these extremes.

What should we do about this? The top anchor, "completely satisfied," would seem to be as strong as we could get. At the other end,

▼ TABLE 7.2 SOME FREQUENCY DISTRIBUTIONS OF CUSTOMER RATINGS

A. Consistently Meeting Quality Expectations

G7	Frequency	Percent	Cumulative frequency	Cumulative percent
1	10	.6	10	.6
2	4	.2	14	.8
3	3	.2	17	1.0
4	3	.2	20	1.2
5	34	2.0	54	3.3
6	13	.8	67	4.0
7	72	4.3	139	8.4
8	299	18.0	438	26.4
9	347	20.9	785	47.3
10	874	52.7	1659	100.0

Mean: 9.07
Median: 9.55

B. Having Access to Applications Engineers

G14	Frequency	Percent	Cumulative frequency	Cumulative percent
1	24	1.7	24	1.7
2	13	.9	37	2.6
3	15	1.1	52	3.7
4	21	1.5	73	5.1
5	111	7.8	184	12.9
6	65	4.6	249	17.5
7	151	10.6	400	28.1
8	347	24.4	747	52.6
9	234	16.5	981	69.0
10	440	31.0	1421	100.0

Mean: 8.18
Median: 8.36

the bottom anchor, "completely dissatisfied," might be too strong. Not many customers that are anywhere near completely dissatisfied on several attributes could be expected to remain with the company. If we softened this term to something such as "not very satisfied" or even "not completely satisfied," perhaps more respondents would give lower ratings and thereby spread ratings along the scale and make it more sensitive. Would this work? We could not be sure unless we ran a test comparing the results from 2 separate, equivalent samples of respondents.

CENTRAL TENDENCY

Most companies want some measure of "central tendency" for each attribute rated. There are 3 types of these measures: mean, median, and mode.

- • • *Mean* is the average score, derived by multiplying each scale point by the number of respondents giving that rating, then summing across all scale points and dividing by the total number of respondents.
- • • *Median* is the midpoint of all ratings, the point on the scale above which there are 50% of the respondent ratings, and the same percentage is below.
- • • *Mode* is the scale point that contains the most responses (e.g., 10 for both scales in Table 7.2).

The mode is seldom used as a measure of customer satisfaction, because it is both unstable and insensitive. Probably most companies use the mean (i.e., average) rating because it is well understood and easy to calculate. However, mean values are not recommended for skewed distributions such as those in Table 7.2, because extreme values such as those at the bottom of the scale tend to drag the calculated mean down and, thereby, exaggerate the influence of lower ratings. A better measure of central tendency for many customer satisfaction attributes is the *median value*, because it is not influenced to any degree by extreme values at either end of the frequency distribution. Therefore, for both scales in Table 7.2, median values should be higher than mean values.

Inspection of Table 7.2 shows that this is indeed the case. The mean for distribution A is 9.07, and the median is slightly higher at 9.55. Similarly, the mean for distribution B is 8.18, and the median is 8.36. Which is the better measure of central tendency for these distributions? Probably the medians, because they are unaffected by extreme ratings or outliers. With so little difference between these measures, it might seem that either could be used, or that the mean could be used because it is easier to calculate and better understood by most people. Perhaps. But when employee compensation is based on cut-offs expressed in 0.1 scale points (e.g., 8.6 or above/below), the choice among measures of central tendency can make a meaningful difference.

Scaling Using Percentages

Instead of measures of central tendency for each attribute, some companies prefer to use the *percentage of ratings* in the top box or top 2 boxes as their measurement scale. Thus, for distribution A, 52.7% of ratings are in the top box (10), and 73.6% are in the top 2 boxes. For distribution B, only 31.0% are in the top box, and 47.5% are in the top 2 boxes. These percentages tend to be higher for verbal scales that go from excellent to poor and even higher for scales from very good to poor.

Scales based on percentages provide a greater range of values from best to worst attributes, and therefore, they could be more sensitive than scaling based on means and medians. They also tend to show high percentages of satisfaction, especially for the top 2 boxes. This makes them more popular with employees at all levels. However, they are based on only 1 or 2 scale points, and they may be too sensitive to the shift of small numbers of cases into or out of these boxes. Nevertheless, percentage scales are widely used because of their simplicity and ease of understanding.

REFERENCES

Devlin, Susan J., H.K. Dong, and Marbue Brown (1993), "Selecting a Scale for Measuring Quality," *Marketing Research*, 5 (3), 12–17.

Haley, Russell I. and Peter B. Case (1979), "Testing Thirteen Attitude Scales for Agreement and Brand Discrimination," *Journal of Marketing*, 43 (Fall), 20–32.

Mullet, Gary M. (1983), "Itemised Rating Scales: Ordinal or Interval?" *European Research*, (April), 49–52.

Myers, James H. and Gregory W. Warner (1968), "Semantic Properties of Selected Evaluation Adjectives,"*Journal of Marketing Research*, 5 (November), 164–68.

Vidali, J. (1955), "Context Effects on Scaled Evaluatory Adjective Meaning," *Journal of the Marketing Research Society*, 17 (1), 21–25.

CHAPTER 8

USING COMPARISON STANDARDS

Thischapter describes a different approach to measuring customer satisfaction. It

- • • Introduces the notion of *comparison standards* in measuring satisfaction,
- • • Shows different ways to measure company performance in relation to customer expectations,
- • • Considers comparison standards other than expectations (e.g., "best competitor," what is "desired"),
- • • Shows some comparisons of results obtained by using different comparison standards with the same respondents, and
- • • Introduces the SERVQUAL instrument for measuring service quality and shows how this concept relates to customer satisfaction.

WHAT ARE COMPARISON STANDARDS?

To this point, the focus has been on single scales for rating company performance only. All scales of this type must reflect the basic principles of sound measurement that are discussed in Chapter 7. It is probably true that most CSM programs are based on single performance rating scales of one kind or another, because these are widely used in market research surveys of various types.

But many people in both the academic and business worlds believe that CSM is different in some important ways from conventional marketing research. In the 1970s, academics became interested in what was then a new concept they called "customer satisfaction." They believed that customers were satisfied only when their prior expectations were met by the products and/or services they purchased; therefore, they defined satisfaction in terms of *meeting customer expectations* (Anderson 1973; Cardozo 1965; Oliver 1980). To the extent that this is true, it suggests that different approaches to measuring customer satisfaction may be required. It implies that company performance should not be measured on an absolute scale but rather in relation to customers' prior expectations. (This is also the standard against which companies are judged when they apply for the annual Baldrige Quality Award.) These expectations can be regarded as *comparison standards*, standards against which company performance is judged or compared (Oliver and Swan 1989; Parasuraman, Berry, and Zeithaml 1990).

Let us start by reviewing the 2 types of customer satisfaction rating scales that involve comparison standards and then showing how results from these scales compare with those for simple performance ratings.

SINGLE EXPECTATIONS/PERFORMANCE SCALES

The 2 basic types of customer satisfaction rating scales presented in Chapter 1 that involve comparison standards based on expectations are single and dual expectations/performance scales.

A typical example of the single expectations/performance scale is as follows:

_____ Exceeded expectations a lot.
_____ Exceeded expectations a little bit.
_____ Met expectations.
_____ Failed expectations a little bit.
_____ Failed expectations a lot.

Dual scaling is discussed later in this chapter.

Let us start by examining some results from a typical single expectations/performance scale and comparing these with performance ratings by the same respondents on the same attributes. This is a good way to see if comparison standards add value or if they produce basically the same information as performance ratings alone. The best way to determine this is to observe how each of these sets of ratings relates to overall satisfaction ratings, because this is the ultimate objective of customer satisfaction programs. And the way to do this is to calculate the average overall rating for each point on a scale for a given attribute and then plot these for all points on the scale, for each attribute in turn. An example will help illustrate.

Simple Performance Versus Meeting Expectations

For a comparison benchmark, Figure 8.1 shows how such a plot would look for a hypothetical attribute that shows no relationship with overall satisfaction. Average overall satisfaction ratings (vertical axis) are the same for each interval on the 10-point scale (horizontal axis), so this attribute has no effect or impact on customer satisfaction. (Readers who are familiar with statistical analysis will recognize that this is simply a "regression line." When such lines are horizontal, as in Figure 8.1, there is no relationship between the 2 variables being plotted.)

▼ **FIGURE 8.1 NO RELATIONSHIP; AVERAGE OVERALL SATISFACTION RATING BY BEING TREATED AS A VALUED CUSTOMER**

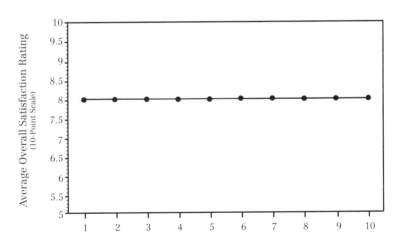

Being Treated as a Valued Customer

Scale: 1 = completely dissatisfied, 10 = completely satisfied.

In contrast, Figure 8.2 shows an actual plot for the attribute "being treated as a valued customer" for performance ratings only on a 10-point scale. For the most part, as ratings increase on this attribute, the corresponding average overall evaluation ratings also increase. This shows that the attribute is clearly related to overall satisfaction and, therefore, is probably one of the factors that affects or drives it. In general, the higher the rating, the higher the overall satisfaction of customers is. There is a small kink in this relationship, in the form of a drop-off in average overall ratings below the 5-scale point, after which there is very little further decline. This could mean that satisfaction drops off noticeably below a rating of 5, or that a rating of 4 is approximately as bad as anything below, or it could be due to the rather small numbers of cases at these low scale points, which make average ratings less stable. In any event, the relationship here is essentially straight-line or *linear* for most scale points.

Now compare these results with those in Figure 8.3, for the single expectations/performance scale. Same attribute, same respondents, same survey questionnaire, same point in time. Here we find quite a different picture. The relationship is clearly *nonlinear* overall, with big

▼**FIGURE 8.2 PERFORMANCE RATING SCALE: AVERAGE OVERALL SATISFACTION RATING BY BEING TREATED AS A VALUED CUSTOMER**

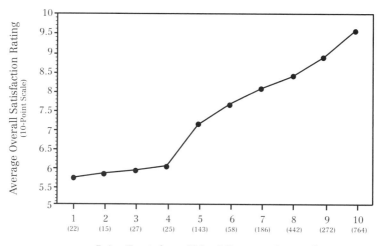

Being Treated as a Valued Customer (respondents)

Scale: 1 = completely dissatisfied, 10 = completely satisfied.

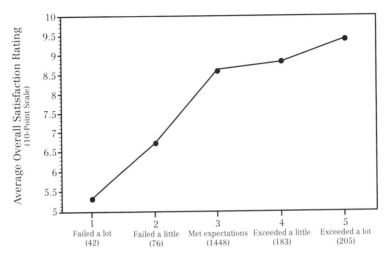

Being Treated as a Valued Customer (respondents)

kinks both below and above the middle point ("met expectations").
These results suggest the following:

• • • "Met expectations" is a respectable rating, with an average overall satisfaction score of approximately 8.7 on the 10-point scale;
• • • Very little is gained even by exceeding customers' expectations "a
lot," and almost nothing is gained by exceeding expectations "a
little";
• • • Failing to meet expectations even "a little" carries a heavy penalty (6.8), much greater than the amount of gain from exceeding expectations "a lot";
• • • Failing to meet expectations "a lot" results in an extreme penalty
(5.3) in terms of overall satisfaction—these are the people who are
most likely to defect and take their business to another supplier.

The results for this attribute do not represent an extreme that was
selected to provide a dramatic illustration. Rather, they are typical for
this particular company. Some other attributes have even steeper
drop-offs for failing to meet expectations even by "a little." An example of this is shown in Figure 8.4, for the attribute "meets after-sales

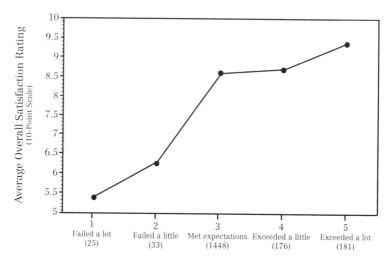

Meets After-Sales Service Expectations (respondents)

service expectations." The penalty here for failing to meet expectations even by "a little" is nearly as severe as failing "a lot." All 20 attributes rated by respondents in this study demonstrated these same basic patterns of results on the single expectations/performance scale.

Meeting Expectations Versus Buying Intention

Brandt's (1988) article provides additional hypothetical examples of how single expectations/performance scales might perform and be interpreted. These examples involved an overnight package delivery service. Assume that customers rated the company on 4 selected attributes using a simple 3-point scale: "not met," "met," and "exceeded expectations." Customers were also asked how likely they would be to select this company for future deliveries. Table 8.1 shows hypothetical results for the 4 attributes. Entries in the table show the *percentage* of respondents at each scale point who said they would "definitely buy again" (whereas the industrial supplier examples presented previously used *average* overall satisfaction ratings).

The first 2 attributes show the same general pattern as that for the industrial supplier: Exceeding expectations gains very little in terms of increasing intentions to buy again, whereas failure to meet expecta-

TABLE 8.1 RELATIONSHIP OF SCALE POINTS TO REPURCHASE INTENT[a]

	Expectations are				
Attribute	**Not met**		**Met**		**Exceeded**
Delivery to all locations	52%	<	80%		86%
Prompt next-day delivery	44	<	75		79
Convenient to use	49		54	<	71
Good at solving problems	39	<	65	<	82

[a]Table entries are percentages of customers who said they would "definitely buy again."
Source: Brandt, D. Randall (1988), "How Service Marketers Can Identify Value-Enhancing Service Elements," *Journal of Services Marketing*, 2 (3), 35–41.

tions results in a severe penalty. Brandt concludes that, for these attributes, it only pays to "hit the target." The next attribute, "convenient to use," shows the opposite pattern, in which exceeding expectations results in a real gain, whereas failing to meet expectations results in little penalty. Finally, the last attribute gives a more symmetrical result, in which exceeding expectations produces a noticeable gain and failing to do so results in a severe penalty. Even though these results are hypothetical, all are entirely possible and have been found in actual surveys.

What this example shows, then, is that different types of rating scales can produce different results and, therefore, interpretations. We can never be sure how the various scale points will relate to outcomes in which we are interested (e.g., overall satisfaction, intention to buy again, actual repurchase). This means that every company should test any measuring scale or scales they are considering by conducting analyses similar to those described previously. These analyses are known as "scale validation," and they tell us how, and how well, the attribute scales are measuring what we want them to measure. Ideally, these comparisons would be performed in a careful pretest before a firm decides on a final questionnaire for ongoing tracking of customer satisfaction.

(As an aside, the preceding examples demonstrate why asking respondents to rate the "importance" of an attribute on a 10-point scale, for example, can be very misleading. Such ratings imply that the relative importance will be the same at every point on the scale for a given attribute. The prior examples show that this often will not be true for every point on the single expectations/performance scale. A better approach is to follow these examples and establish the relative value of each point on the scale more objectively by plotting against some desired outcome measure.)

Frequency Distributions

Another item of interest is the frequency distributions of responses for each of the 2 types of scales (performance only versus single expectations/performance). For example, in Figure 8.3, the numbers of respondents giving each rating are shown in parentheses below the scale point. Note that approximately 75% of all respondents said that this supplier had "met" their expectations in terms of the attention paid to the account. These percentages ranged from 75% to 85% across all attributes in this particular survey, and they suggest that, on balance, most customers were reasonably well satisfied with this industrial supplier. This is not surprising when interviewing present customers. But it is the 42 customers (2%) who said the company had failed "a lot" in terms of attention paid to their accounts that will require special attention. Additional analyses showed that these respondents are far more likely to say they will switch to another supplier, as would be expected.

Conclusions

It seems clear that the single expectations/performance scale produces results that are in the same general direction as those derived from the simple performance-only scale, but the results are also quite different in some ways. The expectations/performance scale more clearly identifies customers that have a high likelihood of leaving the company, and it also shows the severe penalty for failing to meet expectations even by "a little bit." Perhaps equally important, it challenges the conventional wisdom of companies that exhort their employees to *exceed customer expectations*. These efforts usually require much time and money, and they probably will not pay off in this company. We cannot be sure that this holds true for all companies, of course. Each company should test these 2 types of rating scales on its own customers.

Suppose a company finds that its own test results duplicate those provided here. Which of the scales should the company choose? All things considered, the single expectations/performance scale may be better than simple performance ratings for CSM. It is more appropriate to both the academic and the Baldrige Quality Award definitions of satisfaction, it more clearly identifies customers who are most likely to defect, and it offers a way to test the conventional wisdom that calls for exceeding customers' expectations. In the final analysis, each company will have to make its own decision, hopefully based on the results of careful tests and comparisons.

(A note of caution: If a company decides to switch to a single expectations/performance scale from a simple performance rating scale, it is wise to continue using the performance-only scale for several interviewing waves. This will allow comparisons of the performance of the 2 scales over time. It may also provide an opportunity to calibrate the new scale by demonstrating a simple formula to convert ratings on the new scale to those of the old. This can provide continuity by creating a common midpoint and range.)

Prior Expectations Levels

One of the weaknesses of the single expectations/performance scale is that it tells us nothing about customers' prior levels of expectations. These could be uniformly high, low, or somewhere in the middle, but we obtain no information at all about this from a single scale. The reader might think it safe to assume that customer expectations would always be high for most product and/or service categories, but I can think of several categories that seem to produce an unusual degree of frustration among customers or potential customers. These categories might include new and used car dealerships, health-service providers, insurance salespeople and companies, computer hard- and software customer services, and the like. In cases such as these, customers can have their expectations met and still be very dissatisfied!

Conversely, many of us have learned to appreciate some products and services that have been delivered exceptionally well over the years, for the most part. So, when we are asked to rate them on the single expectations/performance scale, we will tend to say that they (only) met our expectations, even though we believe their performance is actually superior. There is no opportunity for us to reflect this in our ratings. It is probably much harder for these products and/or services to exceed our expectations, even by a little bit, than it is for those for which we have much lower expectations.

An example of this is shown in some recent data from INRA (International Research Associates). Figure 8.5 shows average customer satisfaction ratings (performance ratings only) in 7 European countries. Germany was given an index value of 100, and other nations are adjusted in relation to this. Index values range from a high of 162 in Italy to a low of 78 in the Scandinavian countries. Even though the products and/or services surveyed are not completely comparable across countries, there is a good cross-section within the countries. Thus, it seems that there may be some major differences in satisfaction levels among the 7 nations.

How do we explain these variations? They could, of course, be due to the superior performance of business firms in Italy and Spain. How-

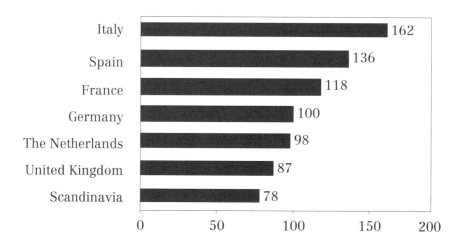

▼ FIGURE 8.5 CUSTOMER SATISFACTION RATINGS IN SEVERAL EUROPEAN COUNTRIES

Italy	162
Spain	136
France	118
Germany	100
The Netherlands	98
United Kingdom	87
Scandinavia	78

0   50   100   150   200

Source: International Research Associates (INRA), courtesy of Haug International Inc.

ever, some of the knowledgeable people who produced these results believe that a more likely explanation is that business performance is actually often lower in those countries, leading to lower expectations among customers. Therefore, performance is evaluated in relation to lower expectations, leading to higher satisfaction with even mediocre performance. Conversely, people in the Scandinavian countries and the United Kingdom generally have much higher expectations, so even a strong performance does not always measure up. The problem, of course, is that we do not know which of these explanations is most accurate because we do not have comparable measures of customers' expectations in the various countries.

DUAL EXPECTATIONS/PERFORMANCE SCALES

One solution to this problem is to ask respondents to give their *prior expectation levels* as well as their performance ratings on 2 separate but parallel scales. This is known as "dual scaling." Here is the example shown in Figure 1.9 in Chapter 1:

Expectations

1   10
Poor   Excellent

Performance

1   10
Poor   Excellent

Because these scales are in juxtaposition, we can easily see if expectations are being met, exceeded, or failed and by how many scale points. We can also see each respondent's prior level of expectations for each attribute. This gives us at least some information as to how much or how little customers expect from this supplier or from all suppliers in a given industry category. Perhaps even more important, it enables us to *track the trends in expectations over time.* This can provide a very valuable insight into whether or not they are rising (they usually are) and, if so, how fast. At the least, it can suggest to a company how fast it will have to move just to stay in place, because in many industries, competitors are conducting their own customer satisfaction programs and constantly making meaningful improvements to their products and/or services.

Another benefit of dual expectations/performance scaling is the greater sensitivity it usually provides. Assuming a 10-point numerical scale with proper anchors (which is often preferred for dual scaling), we can identify places where performance falls short of expectations for as great as 9 points or as little as 1 point. The same is true when performance exceeds expectations. To summarize, dual scaling offers at least 3 advantages over most single expectations/performance scales. It

1. Attempts to measure *absolute levels* of prior expectations as well as current performance,
2. Can track expectation levels over time, and
3. Provides greater scale sensitivity.

However, dual scaling has some drawbacks. Most important is the extra time and effort on the part of the respondent, which results in greater fatigue and, perhaps, a lower response rate in some situations. There is also the possibility of confusion, because most respondents have probably never used scales of this type before (however, this has not been a major problem in many prior market research studies). And finally, because it takes respondents longer to complete their ratings, there is the possibility of added interviewing costs for client companies. Nevertheless, the important advantages may outweigh the disadvantages for many applications. This may be the best of all 4 scaling formats for many companies and situations.

OTHER COMPARISON STANDARDS

To this point, the only comparison standard considered has been customers' *expectations* prior to purchase or use. Even though this was the original standard proposed by academics, it came under attack early on because of its potential logical inconsistencies. Specifically, it makes the assumption that customers' expectations will always be high prior to purchase or use. But what happens when expectations are medium or low for one reason or another and there is no easily available alternative supplier with a superior reputation? In these cases, customers who expect poor service or mediocre merchandise, and whose expectations are met but not exceeded, must be considered satisfied, by definition (LaTour and Peat 1979). Swan and Trawick (1980, p. 11) observe that "it does not seem reasonable to suppose that if a consumer expected a product to perform poorly, and it did so, that the consumer would be satisfied."

Another problem with using expectations as a comparison standard is the uncertain interpretation of the term itself. Does it mean what the customer has *come* to expect? Or what the customer believes he or she has a *right* to expect (e.g., "I expect my supplier/salesperson/doctor to know his or her business, to treat me like a valued customer, or to respond immediately when I need help")? Unless this matter is clarified explicitly in instructions to respondents, we will not know which interpretation they are using. Any repeat customer who goes into a McDonald's restaurant or opens a can of Coke or a box of Tide knows exactly what to expect, so it is hard to see how expectations can be useful in the case of frequently purchased products and/or services such as these.

All of this has led to a rethinking of the construct of customer satisfaction and to alternative comparison standards for measuring it. Miller (1977) saw the potential for several possible alternative interpretations of the term "expectations," including

• • • *Ideal expectations*, the "wished for" level of performance, or what performance can be;
• • • *Expected expectations*, based on past averaged performance, or what the performance probably will be (might also be called "predicted" performance);

- • • *Minimum tolerable expectations*, the lowest acceptable level of performance ("better than nothing"), or what performance must be; and
- • • *Deserved expectations*, based on the customer's investment of time and money, or what performance should be.

However, he did not test any of these options. More recently, Olshavsky and Spreng (1989) have proposed a new model of consumer satisfaction in which desires, not expectations, are assumed to be the appropriate comparison standard. This same point of view was put forth previously by other writers (Sirgy 1984; Swan and Trawick 1980; Woodruff, Cadotte, and Jenkins 1983). Westbrook and Reilly (1983) tested both expectations and desires as comparison standards. They did not find that desires were superior to expectations, but they suggested that this might have been due to measurement problems.

In an attempt at clarification, Zeithaml, Berry, and Parasuraman (1993) conducted 16 focus groups in 5 widely scattered cities for a diverse set of service categories (e.g., insurance, business equipment repair, hotels). Broad, open-ended questions were asked in a nondirective and unstructured fashion; for example, "What do you expect from a service provider?" "Have your expectations changed over time?" and "Where do your expectations come from?" From these groups, they were able to develop a model of service expectations that specified 3 different levels of customer expectations:

1. *Desired service,* or what customers want;
2. *Adequate service*, or what customers are willing to accept; and
3. *Predicted service*, or what customers believe is likely to occur.

From all of the preceding, it is easy to see the great amount of confusion that exists in the meaning of the term "expectation." It is also possible that this meaning may vary from one product and/or service category to another. Perhaps the proper conclusion is that *whenever the term "expectations" is used in either single or dual expectations/performance scaling, its exact meaning should be defined carefully for respondents.* It is the responsibility of the questionnaire designer to see that this is done clearly.

Comparisons of Alternative Comparison Standards

Spreng and Olshavsky (1993) compare both expectations and desires as comparison standards in a single study. They find that meeting customers' desires had a significant effect on overall satisfaction but meeting expectations did not. In another study, Spreng, MacKenzie, and Olshavsky (1996) also compare expectations and desires as comparison standards. They find low correlations between respondent ratings on these standards, leading them to conclude that "desires and expectations are empirically distinct" (p. 27). They also find that though both expectations and desires disconfirmation affected overall satisfaction, "it is clear that the impact of desires congruency was at least as great as the impact of expectations congruency, and there is some evidence that the impact of desires congruency was even greater" (p. 25).

Myers (1991) compares the performance of 2 comparison standards, *expected* and *wanted*, among people who had recently purchased a new car. (Figure 8.6 shows the first page of the questionnaire.) They were asked to rate, on 20 attributes, one of the dealerships (chosen at random) at which they shopped. For each attribute, they were asked how much they *wanted* it, how much they had *expected* a priori to get it, and how much they believed they actually *got* that attribute from the selected dealership, whether or not they bought a car from the dealer. The "got" ratings were subtracted from the "wanted" ratings to obtain the percentage of respondents with a "wanted deficiency" (wanted – got = wanted deficiency), and the same for the "expected" ratings. Results are shown in Table 8.2, arranged by similar statement groupings from a factor analysis. For 14 of the 20 attributes, "wanted ratings" were higher than "expected" ratings; for 2 attributes, both ratings were approximately equal; and for 4 attributes, "expectations" ratings were higher. Myers (1991, p. 41) concluded,

> On balance, then, respondents were much more likely to *want more than they expected* from new car dealers than the reverse. An important point is that wants were different from expected standards for 18 of the 20 attributes.... Clearly, those 2 comparison standards are measuring somewhat different concepts or ideas.

Because the 2 comparison standards produced different results, it is important to know which was more highly related to overall satisfaction with the dealership. "Wanted" minus "got" ratings (W – G) had a correlation of .26 with overall satisfaction, versus .18 for "expectations" minus "got" (E – G). The multiple correlation of "wanted" minus "got" scores versus overall satisfaction across all 20 attributes was .64, compared with .52 for "expectations." Myers (1991, p. 41) concluded that "if these findings are confirmed by other studies, business firms should seriously consider using 'wanted' or 'desired' rather

▼ FIGURE 8.6 QUESTIONNAIRE

Below are several benefits you might have wanted when you shopped for your new car recently. For <u>each</u> of the benefits shown, please indicate the following:

• • • How much you EXPECTED the dealer to offer that benefit
• • • How much you WANTED that benefit
• • • How much you GOT that benefit from the dealer

Please circle your answers on the 10-point scale. Make sure you circle a number for each EXPECTED line, WANTED line, and GOT line for each benefit, to show how you feel about each.

		Not at all	Extremely	Doesn't apply
Sufficient parking space for my car	Expected from dealer	1 2 3 4 5 6 7 8 9 10		x
	Wanted from dealer	1 2 3 4 5 6 7 8 9 10		x
	Got from dealer	1 2 3 4 5 6 7 8 9 10		x
Attractive showroom	Expected from dealer	1 2 3 4 5 6 7 8 9 10		x
	Wanted from dealer	1 2 3 4 5 6 7 8 9 10		x
	Got from dealer	1 2 3 4 5 6 7 8 9 10		x
Open evenings or Saturdays for service	Expected from dealer	1 2 3 4 5 6 7 8 9 10		x
	Wanted from dealer	1 2 3 4 5 6 7 8 9 10		x
	Got from dealer	1 2 3 4 5 6 7 8 9 10		x
Had many models or types of car in stock	Expected from dealer	1 2 3 4 5 6 7 8 9 10		x
	Wanted from dealer	1 2 3 4 5 6 7 8 9 10		x
	Got from dealer	1 2 3 4 5 6 7 8 9 10		x
Had many colors and options of same models	Expected from dealer	1 2 3 4 5 6 7 8 9 10		x
	Wanted from dealer	1 2 3 4 5 6 7 8 9 10		x
	Got from dealer	1 2 3 4 5 6 7 8 9 10		x
Carried more than one brand of car	Expected from dealer	1 2 3 4 5 6 7 8 9 10		x
	Wanted from dealer	1 2 3 4 5 6 7 8 9 10		x
	Got from dealer	1 2 3 4 5 6 7 8 9 10		x
Salesperson was polite and courteous	Expected from dealer	1 2 3 4 5 6 7 8 9 10		x
	Wanted from dealer	1 2 3 4 5 6 7 8 9 10		x
	Got from dealer	1 2 3 4 5 6 7 8 9 10		x

	Percent Deficiency	
Factor	Expected	Wanted
I Personal Interest		
Answered my questions clearly	47	62
Dealer you can trust	44	66
Effort to know my needs	47	54
Explained terms of sale	40	51
Salesperson polite and courteous	34	45
Didn't avoid my questions	34	48
Good service department	48	59
II Merchandise Assortment		
Many models or types in stock	51	55
Many colors and options	59	65
Open evenings or Saturday for service	43	50
III Terms of Sale		
Good interest rates	30	40
Fair price for trade-in	30	40
Price very competitive	37	52
IV Physical Facilities		
Sufficient parking space	42	43
Attractive showroom	39	29
V Car Features		
Made comparisons with other makes	50	43
More than one brand of car	14	15
Pointed out many features of car	49	44
VI No High Pressure		
Did not high pressure me	50	34
Called afterward to check my satisfaction	33	40

than 'expectations' as comparison standards in measuring customer satisfaction."

It is clear from the preceding discussion that (1) many writers have recognized the shortcomings of the term "expectations" as a comparison standard; (2) there is a need for a standard that is higher than expectations; and (3) "ideal" performance might be the answer, but it has proven very difficult to operationalize (Holbrook 1984; Tse and Wilton 1988; Wilkie and Pessemier 1973). The limited evidence available suggests that *either desires or wants may be superior to expectations as a comparison standard for most customer satisfaction surveys*. It gives a respondent the chance to go beyond the status quo and indicate any "overexpected" performance that would really be preferred or appreciated. It also does not lead to the logical inconsistencies inherent in the expectations standards that were discussed previously.

Why Use Comparison Standards?

After reading the preceding, some might ask, "Why use comparison standards at all, in view of the various uncertainties and options? Why not just use simple performance ratings and avoid the uncertainties involved with comparison standards?" The answer is that every scale *needs* a comparison standard, and in fact, every scale *has* a comparison standard. To illustrate, suppose you are asked what an average rating of 6.0 on a particular attribute means, how it should be interpreted. You will not be able to answer that question until you know how many points or intervals the entire scale contains. If it is 6, you will give one interpretation; if it is 10, you will give another. Therefore, the 6 and 10 are de facto comparison standards.

In general, the "top box" on any scale (e.g., 10 on a 10-point scale, 7 on a 7-point scale) is the only comparison standard that is available in the case of single performance ratings. We might call these *implicit* standards, because they are not values given by respondents. The problem is that these top box standards are the same for every respondent and every attribute, and they imply that all respondents are the same and that all want or expect the maximum possible on each attribute. Is this realistic? I personally doubt it, and I have considerable evidence from my own work, as well as others', to indicate that this is not normally the case.

In contrast, comparison standards such as expected/desired/wanted enable respondents to indicate amounts that can vary from attribute to attribute and from person to person. We might call these *explicit* comparison standards. In this perspective, then, the choice is not between using or not using comparison standards. There will always be comparison standards. The choice is between using implicit or explicit standards for CSM. A considerable body of experience and research among both companies and academics suggests that *explicit comparison standards can be very helpful in measuring customer satisfaction.* They clearly provide additional data and different perspectives than those available from the simple performance ratings that are typical of most marketing research surveys and also of much CSM.

THE SERVQUAL INSTRUMENT

Any discussion of dual scaling using comparison standards would not be complete without reference to a widely used measuring instrument developed in the mid-1980s to measure service quality. This instrument is known as SERVQUAL. It was developed in 1985 by 3 marketing scholars, A. Parasuraman, Valarie Zeithaml, and Leonard Berry, to measure the perceived quality of a service experience. (Zeithaml [1986, p. 1] notes that "by perceived quality, we mean the consumer's judgment about a product's overall excellence or superiority.") These writers observe:

> Few academic researchers have attempted to define and model quality because of the difficulties in delimiting and measuring the construct. Moreover, despite the phenomenal growth of the service sector, only a handful of these researchers have focused on service quality.... Knowledge about goods' quality, however, is insufficient to understand service quality. Three well-documented characteristics of service—*intangibility, heterogeneity,* and *inseparability*—must be acknowledged for a full understanding of service quality. (Parasuraman, Zeithaml, and Berry 1985, p. 41)

Service quality and customer satisfaction are probably closely related constructs. Some believe that the term "quality" is a label that applies to or describes a product and/or service itself, whereas "satisfaction" is a subjective reaction or evaluation on the part of a consumer of the product and/or service (Bitner and Hubbert 1994; Dabholkar 1993). Others believe that service quality is a long-term attitude, but consumer satisfaction is a "transitory" judgment made on the basis of a specific service encounter (Cronin and Taylor 1992; Oliver 1993; Patterson and Johnson 1993). Whatever the conceptual distinctions, the 2 concepts are almost surely highly related empirically. High quality (whatever its precise meaning) usually produces high satisfaction, and vice versa. In practice, the term "quality" often is used as a substitute or proxy for the term "customer satisfaction" (e.g., as in a high-quality meal, car, clothing item, or travel experience).

To the extent that these 2 concepts are similar, the SERVQUAL measuring instrument (or a variation of it) could easily be adapted to measure customer satisfaction in a wide variety of service industries, and even in some product industries. This instrument was developed by interviewing 200 adult respondents who were users of any of 5 types of services: appliance repair and maintenance, retail banking, long-distance telephone, securities brokerage, or credit cards. The sample included 40 recent users of each type. Ratings were given on nearly 100 specific aspects of service quality. Analysis of these ratings showed that these aspects fell into only 5 major topic categories:

• • • Tangibility,
• • • Reliability,
• • • Responsiveness,
• • • Assurance, and
• • • Empathy.

A detailed explanation of the methodology and findings can be found in Parasuraman, Zeithaml, and Berry (1988). The result of this work was a 34-item instrument that can be used to measure service quality (and perhaps customer satisfaction) in a wide variety of service industries.

Defining the Comparison Standard

For our purposes, we are especially interested in the definition of a comparison standard for measuring service quality and how this might differ from a comparison standard for measuring customer satisfaction. Parasuraman, Zeithaml, and Berry (1986, p. 6) state that

> The term "expectations" as used in the service quality literature differs from expectations as used in the consumer satisfaction literature. Specifically, in the satisfaction literature, expectations are viewed as *predictions* made by consumers about what is likely to happen during an impending transaction or exchange.... In contrast, in the service quality literature, expectations are viewed as desires or wants of consumers, i.e., what they feel a service provider *should* rather than *would* offer.

Therefore, all their measurements of quality in different service industries define expectations in terms of what the provider should do; for example, "Please show the extent to which you think firms offering _____ services should possess the features described by each statement" (Parasuraman, Zeithaml, and Berry 1986, p. 31).

Comment

It is clear from the preceding that a great deal of controversy surrounds the use of expectations as a comparison standard in measuring either customer satisfaction or service quality. Some academics feel strongly that explicit comparison standards should not be used at all; simple performance ratings are sufficient (see Cronin and Taylor 1992; Peter, Churchill, and Brown 1993; Teas 1994). Although many disagree and believe they should be used, there is a considerable amount of confusion and disagreement over exactly how to word the comparison standard, as we have seen. And some writers believe that satisfaction cannot be measured adequately without using both desires and expectations as comparison standards (Spreng, MacKenzie, and Olshavsky 1996).

It may be best to think of a comparison standard as adding another dimension in the measurement of customer satisfaction. Even if it is true that performance ratings alone can measure overall customer satisfaction as well as, or even better than, the gap between the comparison standard and rated performance (as maintained by many writers), a comparison standard can still add value in several ways:

1. It allows a company to track expectations/desires/wants and so forth over time, for use in future planning;
2. The gap between performance and the comparison standard can indicate areas that need immediate improvement much more clearly than performance ratings alone; and
3. If desires or wants are used as the comparison standard, any gaps between these ratings and corresponding performance ratings for any attribute can spotlight opportunities for new or greatly improved products or services.[1]

And, of course, the performance ratings portion of dual expectations/performance rating scales can always be used to establish basic levels of satisfaction in the usual manner. It is my feeling that companies that make the effort to include a carefully defined comparison standard in a customer satisfaction questionnaire will find it useful in many ways.

---

[1] I have used these "need-gaps" in exactly this way for more than 20 years. Products such as the Kodak Advantix camera and Frito-Lay's Sun Chips came from studies conducted to identify unmet needs in these product categories.

REFERENCES

Anderson, Rolph E. (1973), "Consumer Dissatisfaction: The Effect of Disconfirmed Expectancy on Perceived Product Performance," *Journal of Marketing Research*, 10 (February), 38–44.

Bitner, Mary Jo and Amy R. Hubbert (1994), "Encounter Satisfaction Versus Overall Satisfaction Versus Quality: The Customer's Voice," in *Service Quality: New Directions in Theory and Practice*, Roland T. Rust and Richard L. Oliver, eds. Thousand Oaks, CA: Sage Publications, 72–94.

Brandt, D. Randall (1988), "How Service Marketers Can Identify Value-Enhancing Service Elements," *Journal of Services Marketing*, 2 (3), 35–41.

Cardozo, Richard N. (1965), "An Experimental Study of Customer Effort, Expectation, and Satisfaction," *Journal of Marketing Research*, 2 (August), 244–49.

Cronin, J. Joseph, Jr. and Steven A. Taylor (1992), "Measuring Service Quality: A Re-Examination and Extension," *Journal of Marketing*, 56 (July), 55–68.

Dabholkar, Pratibha A. (1993), "Customer Satisfaction and Service Quality: Two Constructs or One?" in *Enhancing Knowledge Development in Marketing*, Vol. 4, David W. Cravens and Peter Dickson, eds. Chicago: American Marketing Association, 10–18.

Holbrook, Morris B. (1984), "Situation-Specific Ideal Points and Usage of Multiple Dissimilar Brands," in *Research in Marketing*, Vol. 7, Jagdish N. Sheth, ed. Greenwich, CT: JAI Press Inc., 93–112.

LaTour, Steven A. and Nancy C. Peat (1979), "Conceptual and Methodological Issues in Consumer Satisfaction Research," in *Advances in Consumer Research*, Vol. 6, William L. Wilkie, ed. Ann Arbor, MI: Association for Consumer Research, 431–37.

Miller, John A. (1977), "Studying Satisfaction, Modifying Models, Eliciting Expectations, Posing Problems, and Making Meaningful Measurements," in *Conceptualization and Measurement of Consumer Satisfaction and Dissatisfaction*, No. 77–103, H. Keith Hunt, ed. Cambridge, MA: Marketing Science Institute Report, 72–89.

Myers, James H. (1991), "Measuring Customer Satisfaction: Is Meeting Expectations Enough?" *Marketing Research*, 3 (December), 35–43.

Oliver, Richard L. (1980), "A Cognitive Model of the Antecedents and Consequences of Satisfaction Decisions," *Journal of Marketing Research*, 17 (November), 460–69.

―――― (1993), "A Conceptual Model of Service Quality and Service Satisfaction: Compatible Goals, Different Concepts," in *Advances in Services Marketing and Management*, Vol. 2, Teresa A. Swartz,

David A. Bowen, and Stephen W. Brown, eds. Greenwich, CT: JAI Press, 65–85.

——— and John E. Swan (1989), "Equity and Disconfirmation Perceptions as Influences on Merchant and Product Satisfaction," *Journal of Consumer Research*, 16 (December), 372–83.

Olshavsky, Richard W. and Richard A. Spreng (1989), "A 'Desires as Standard' Model of Consumer Satisfaction," *Journal of Consumer Satisfaction, Dissatisfaction and Complaining Behavior*, 2, 49–54.

Parasuraman, A., Leonard L. Berry, and Valarie A. Zeithaml (1990), "Guidelines for Conducting Service Quality Research," *Marketing Research*, 2 (December), 34–44.

———, Valarie A. Zeithaml, and Leonard L. Berry (1985), "A Conceptual Model of Service Quality and Its Implications for Future Research," *Journal of Marketing*, 49 (Fall), 41–50.

———, ———, and ——— (1986), "SERVQUAL: A Multiple-Item Scale for Measuring Customer Perceptions of Service Quality," *Report No. 86–108*. Cambridge, MA: Marketing Science Institute.

———, ———, and ——— (1988), "SERVQUAL: A Multiple-Item Scale for Measuring Consumer Perceptions of Service Quality," *Journal of Retailing*, 64 (Spring), 12–40.

Patterson, Paul G. and Lester W. Johnson (1993), "Disconfirmation of Expectations and the Gap Model of Service Quality: An Integrated Paradigm," *Journal of Consumer Satisfaction, Dissatisfaction, and Complaining Behavior*, 6.

Peter, J. Paul, Gilbert A. Churchill, Jr., and Tom J. Brown (1993), "Caution in the Use of Difference Scores in Consumer Research," *Journal of Consumer Research*, 19 (March), 655–62.

Sirgy, Joseph M. (1984), "A Social Cognition Model of Consumer Satisfaction/Dissatisfaction," *Psychology and Marketing,* 1 (Summer), 27–43.

Spreng, Richard A., Scott B. MacKenzie, and Richard W. Olshavsky (1996), "A Reexamination of the Determinants of Consumer Satisfaction," *Journal of Marketing*, 60 (July), 15–32.

——— and Richard W. Olshavsky (1993), "A Desires Congruency Model of Consumer Satisfaction," *Journal of the Academy of Marketing Science*, 21 (Summer), 169–77.

Swan, John E. and I. Frederick Trawick (1980), "Satisfaction Related to Predictive Vs. Desired Expectations," in *Refining Concepts and Measures of Consumer Satisfaction and Complaining Behavior*, H. Keith Hunt and Ralph L. Day, eds. Bloomington, IN: Indiana University, 7–12.

Teas, R. Kenneth (1994), "Expectations as a Comparison Standard in Measuring Service Quality: An Assessment of a Reassessment," *Journal of Marketing*, 58 (January), 132–39.

Tse, David K. and Peter C. Wilton (1988), "Models of Consumer Satisfaction Formation: An Extension," *Journal of Marketing Research*, 25 (May), 204–12.

Westbrook, Robert A. and Michael D. Reilly (1983), "Value-Percept Disparity: An Alternative to the Disconfirmation of Expectations Theory of Consumer Satisfaction" in *Advances in Consumer Research*, Vol. 10, Richard P. Bagozzi and Alice M. Tybout, eds. Ann Arbor, MI: Association for Consumer Research, 256–61.

Wilkie, William L. and Edgar A. Pessemier (1973), "Issues in Marketing's Use of Multi-Attribute Attitude Models," *Journal of Marketing Research*, 10 (November), 428–41.

Woodruff, Robert B., Ernest R. Cadotte, and Roger L. Jenkins (1983), "Modeling Consumer Satisfaction Processes Using Experience-Based Norms," *Journal of Marketing Research*, 20 (August), 296–304.

Zeithaml, Valarie A. (1986), "Defining and Relating Price, Perceived Quality, and Perceived Value," working paper, Department of Marketing, Duke University.

———, Leonard L. Berry, and A. Parasuraman (1993), "The Nature and Determinants of Customer Expectations of Service," *Journal of the Academy of Marketing Science*, 21, 1–12.

CHAPTER 9

OTHER MEASUREMENT ISSUES

I n this chapter, we examine a variety of additional measurement issues that should always be considered when designing a customer satisfaction program. These include

• • • Looking for *strategic breakpoints* that show more clearly where to focus improvement efforts;

• • • Assessing the *market damage* of specific problems that cause customers to defect;

• • • Increasing *rating scale sensitivity* to provide maximum opportunity for "moving the needle" from one survey wave to the next;

• • • Testing for real, *statistically significant differences* in mean or median customer ratings from one time period to another;

• • • Comparing the company's satisfaction ratings to those of its competitors, especially to the "best in class," for *benchmarking* purposes; and

• • • Understanding the importance of *reliability and validity* in designing a questionnaire.

All of these can contribute to a more coherent and useful CSM program. As was pointed out previously, results from these programs often get far more careful scrutiny than most market research studies, so it is worth spending extra time to get them right.

STRATEGIC BREAKPOINTS

One type of analysis that is especially useful in customer satisfaction research is to look for "breakpoints" in the relationships between attribute measures and some desired outcome measure (e.g., overall satisfaction, switching behavior or likelihood, repurchase rates). There are examples of this in Chapter 8 with plotting average overall satisfaction scores for each scale point for selected attributes. Recall that Figure 8.2 shows a small breakpoint below the 5-scale point on a 10-point, performance-only scale. Figure 8.3 shows a much sharper breakpoint below the "met expectations" rating on the single expectations/performance scale. Because these are based on the analysis of respondent ratings, we might call them *subjective* breakpoints. Every company can look for patterns of this type when analyzing survey results, using the approach illustrated in Chapter 8.

Similarly, it is often possible to deal with *objective* measures of one kind or another (e.g., time, cost) when surveying customers. For example, one fast-food restaurant chain was concerned that the amount of time elapsed between placing and receiving an order might affect customer satisfaction. What the chain found was that this time interval had no effect on customer satisfaction—up to 5 minutes. After 5 minutes of waiting time, the interval became increasingly important. This was the breakpoint the company could not exceed without having an effect on satisfaction. We might call this an *objective* breakpoint.

Several additional examples of objective breakpoints are provided by Finkleman (1993) of the McKinsey Customer Satisfaction Practice. Figure 9.1 shows how he conceptualizes breakpoints in terms of a "zone of indifference," in which some objective factor has the greatest impact on customer satisfaction and/or loyalty. Below and above this zone, the factor has little effect on loyalty. The shape of such a relationship can vary widely from one category to another, of course, and some categories might have only a negative or a positive breakpoint, but not both.

Figure 9.2 shows 2 examples of objective breakpoints involving time delays. Satisfaction is shown on the vertical axis in terms of the percentage who say they would repurchase. The relationship for bank tellers looks very similar to the 5-minute delay for the fast-food restaurant mentioned previously. Waiting times up to 4 minutes for bank tellers have little effect on customer satisfaction; beyond that, satis-

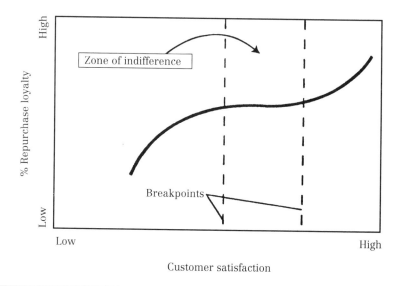

Source: Finkleman, Daniel (1993), "Crossing the 'Zone of Indifference'," *Marketing Management*, 2 (3), 22–31.

faction drops sharply up to 8 minutes. After 8 minutes, satisfaction continues to drop but at a much slower rate. Similarly, satisfaction is not greatly affected by a computer downtime of up to approximately 4 hours, then it drops sharply to 6 hours, then it drops very little after that. In both examples, the drop in satisfaction is dramatic in the zone of indifference.

Figure 9.3 shows some breakpoints for automobile service, as revealed by the J.D. Power Customer Satisfaction Index (obtained after 1 year of ownership). Here, the zone of indifference is between 35–40% repair comeback rate. Above that, customer satisfaction declines from almost 100% for a minimal 15% comeback rate to approximately 85% at a 35% comeback rate. (This is one reason why Lexus is usually first in the J.D. Power Satisfaction Index.) Above a 40% comeback rate, satisfaction drops much more rapidly than below a 35% rate. In this range, increasing the repair comeback rate even 5% has a major effect on satisfaction ratings.

Comment

All of these examples suggest that there are likely to be breakpoints—either subjective, objective, or both—in many product and/or

▼ FIGURE 9.2 BREAKPOINTS FOR COMPUTER SYSTEMS AND BANK TELLERS

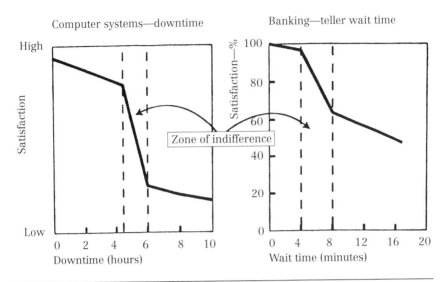

Source: Finkleman, Daniel (1993), "Crossing the 'Zone of Indifference'," *Marketing Management*, 2 (3), 22–31.

service categories. It is important to note that *these will not be obvious in the normal course of most satisfaction research data analysis,* yet they can alert companies to specific points at which satisfaction goes quickly from good to bad and bad to worse. This is where efforts need to be focused, not at points outside the zone of indifference. Therefore, as many objective measures as possible should be taken, and all measures should be analyzed carefully for breakpoints, using objective, statistical methods such as those described previously.

Another way to establish strategic breakpoints is subjective in nature and asks respondents to indicate their own feelings in a survey format. One way would be to ask each respondent to indicate a point in time (or other objective measure), or even an interval on a rating scale, at which performance starts to become unacceptable to them. Alternatively, the interviewer could read to the respondent *each point* on whatever scale is being considered. The respondent would indicate whether that scale point is acceptable or unacceptable. Or, the respondent could indicate the *degree of acceptability* of each interval on the scale, using a scale of acceptability (e.g., 10 = Completely acceptable, 1 = Not at all acceptable). However, none of these "direct" methods may be as accurate as the "indirect" methods illustrated in the preceding figures.

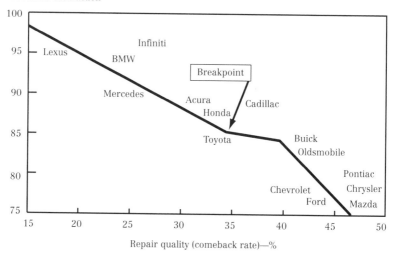

Source: Finkleman, Daniel (1993), "Crossing the 'Zone of Indifference'," *Marketing Management*, 2 (3), 22–31.

The existing evidence suggests that CSM is full of potential strategic breakpoints, both subjective and objective. (The same might also be true in market research generally, but many investigators do not look carefully for them or do not measure them properly.) These breakpoints might be even more useful for planning purposes than are "benchmarks" from leading competitors. The primary reason is that *breakpoints are based on customers themselves*, rather than on possibly suboptimal practices adopted arbitrarily by even the best competitors. Strategic breakpoints can usually be found rather easily with the proper kind of analysis.

MARKET DAMAGE

Not everyone sees CSM programs in a favorable light. The Technical Assistance Research Programs (TARP) company has identified 3 primary problems with programs it has seen in working with more than 400 major corporations in North America, Japan, and Europe (Goodman, Broetzmann, and Adamson 1992):

1. Companies cannot interpret the meaning of the dissatisfaction measure.

2. Very few companies include questions about "market actions" for different satisfaction levels.
3. Customers are not usually asked about the sources of their satisfaction or dissatisfaction.

There is not enough space here to expand upon these points, but Goodman, Broetzmann, and Adamson (1992, p. 35–37) do so in their article. They also present a "five-step core group approach to strategically improving a company's ability to satisfy customers" (p. 37). One of these steps is especially interesting because it focuses on the *market actions* of different satisfaction levels found in customer surveys. Goodman, Broetzmann, and Adamson note,

> How can you calculate the market impact of improved quality and service? Basically, you need five pieces of data:
>
> 1. The long-term profit value of a customer
> 2. The number of customers who experience problems
> 3. The effect that problems have on customers' loyalty
> 4. The effect of your service system on loyalty
> 5. The percentage of customers who bother to complain about problems
>
> With these data, you can quantify the return on investment of problem prevention, enhanced service accessibility, and improved satisfaction with service. (p. 37)

They present the following example of how to calculate return on investment for a company that sells widgets. Assume that each customer will buy a widget once a year at a profit of $25 per year. Assume also that the total number of sales lost last year can be broken down into 2 components: those lost because of some kind of problem (preventable) and those lost but not because of a problem (not preventable). A customer survey is needed to determine or estimate these numbers. Then, the latter number is subtracted from the total number of sales lost to get the number of lost sales that were preventable.

All that remains is to multiply this number by the $25 profit per sale to obtain the total amount of profit lost annually because of problems that were preventable by the company. Goodman, Broetzmann, and Adamson give the following illustration:

$$63,590 \text{ sales lost because of problems}$$
$$\underline{\times \$25 \text{ profit per customer}}$$
$$\$1,589,750 \text{ profits lost because of problems}$$

Using these figures as a baseline, TARP estimates the amount a company would reduce its preventable losses by any particular program (e.g., an 800-number to handle complaint calls) it installs to improve satisfaction among customers. It also calculates a return on investment for each improvement program on the basis of its cost and estimated additional annual profits. TARP points out:

> The market damage method can also effectively address the fact that not all problems cause an equal amount of market damage and that market damage should be the key factor in setting priorities for quality improvement. At the moment, most companies set priorities based on the squeaky wheel approach—when enough complaints come in or when someone reaches the CEO, action will be taken. (p. 38)

After the market damage for each type of problem has been computed, problems can be ranked according to overall market damage and addressed in that order.

> Improving existing systems involves redesigning the customer service and complaint handling systems to achieve two key goals: to do the job right the first time, thereby avoiding complaints, and to have an effective complaint management system that gets all unhappy customers to articulate their dissatisfaction so that companies can win back their loyalty and identify why problems occurred so they can be prevented. (p. 38)

TARP finds that, using this example, the loss of approximately $1.5 million was due to 54% of the customers experiencing a problem and only 45% complaining. Of those that complained, only 31% were satisfied with the treatment they received.

Comment

Although conventional CSM and TARP both focus on identifying weaknesses in a company's offerings, TARP identifies more specific problems and problem areas, calculates lost profits due to customers who leave, estimates the additional annual profit from specific programs intended to reduce lost sales, and calculates the return on investment from each program. All this can identify specific areas that need improvement and indicate probable savings amounts. This enables management to decide how many resources can justifiably be spent on improving each problem area and all areas combined. The focus is on problems, not on subjective evaluations of satisfaction.

MOVING THE NEEDLE

A common problem in CSM programs is one that might be called "moving the needle." It occurs because most meaningful programs are based on repeated surveys of samples of customers, usually at intervals of 3 to 6 months, and any changes that are found tend to be minimal. This could be due, at least in part, to rating scale insensitivity. Management is naturally interested in trends of all measures over time, including overall satisfaction, specific attributes, likelihood of switching to another supplier, willingness to recommend to others, and the like. However, insensitive rating scales can create several problems when looking for trends over time.

• • • Trends are hard to establish when surveys are done only every 3 to 6 months;
• • • The shorter the interval between interviewing waves, the less likely it is that any real internal change has occurred;
• • • Any changes that are found are so small that they are unlikely to be statistically significant, yet in some systems, cut-off points are established that determine the compensation of employees, even at upper management levels. (Should changes in compensation be based on differences that are *not* statistically significant?);
• • • Employees, at all levels, who are focusing on improving one or more aspects of their product and/or service often see little or no immediate change in their ratings; and
• • • Management becomes frustrated that customer satisfaction improvement targets are not met quickly at statistically significant levels of confidence.

Some of these problems are simply inherent in customer satisfaction tracking programs. (In contrast, most conventional market research consists of one-time projects, except for short-term advertising tracking studies, which have some of the same problems.) What all of this comes down to is the question of how much of a change in survey measures should be considered a *real* change, and how much is more likely due to chance fluctuations from one sample to another. There is no simple solution to this problem, but there are ways of ameliorating it to some extent. One way is by *scaling*, another is by *statistical analysis*.

Scaling Considerations

One way to increase scale sensitivity so that ratings change more from one interviewing wave to the next is to do whatever possible to increase the *dispersion or range* of attribute ratings. Several methods of doing this have been discussed in previous chapters, including

• • • *Lengthening* the scale; other things being equal, a 10-point scale will usually spread ratings at least a little better than a 5-point scale (but probably not double the amount);

• • • *Strengthening* both lower and upper anchor statements (on a numerical scale) or the top- and bottom-box descriptors (on a verbal scale); or

• • • Using an *unbalanced* scale that has more intervals above the neutral point than below.

These and other steps can help spread ratings on scales for individual attributes or overall satisfaction ratings. The same is true for likelihood of switching, willingness to recommend company to others, and other meaningful measures. Often, the problem is simply too few scale points (e.g., 4 or 5). Scales this short may be adequate for market research, but they are probably much too short for sensitive CSM. This is especially true when interviewing present customers, most of whom are reasonably satisfied, or they would not be customers. In these cases, most ratings will tend to fall in the top box or top 2 boxes (unless the scale is carefully constructed). We saw examples of this in Chapter 7. Such scales cannot be as sensitive as those that spread ratings over 5 to 7 scale points in a 7- or 10-point scale.

Statistical Considerations

From a statistical standpoint, one easy way to increase sensitivity, of course, is to *increase sample sizes* greatly for each interviewing wave. This will decrease the sampling error to the point at which even small changes in ratings have a much better chance of being statistically significant. However, this obviously adds great expense. Also, many companies (especially business-to-business) do not have enough customers to enable them to do this. About all that can be said is that survey waves should cover as many customers as possible and as frequently as possible, within sampling and budget constraints.

Another way to reduce the sampling error is to *interview the same customers in each survey wave*. Of course, it may not be practical or desirable to bother the same customers over and over again, but if it is, this will substantially reduce the sampling error and lower the size of the change in ratings required for statistical significance. This comes about because of the statistical correlation between the 2 sets of ratings that are given by the same person.

The usual formula for testing the significance of differences between 2 means of independent samples of respondents (e.g., Wave 1 versus Wave 2) on any survey measure is

$$Z = \overline{X}_2 - \overline{X}_1/se_{d\overline{x}},$$

where

$\overline{X}_1, \overline{X}_2$ = mean ratings on any attribute or on overall satisfaction ratings for Wave 1 and Wave 2,

$se_{d\overline{x}}$ = standard error of the difference between *independent* means,

= $\sqrt{s_{\overline{x}_1}^2 + s_{\overline{x}_2}^2}$ and $s_x = [s/(\sqrt{N} - 1)]$, and

s = standard deviations of each set of ratings.

However, when the same respondents are interviewed in both waves, the formula for the standard error of difference between *correlated* means becomes

$$se_{d\overline{x}} = \sqrt{s_{\overline{x}_1}^2 + s_{\overline{x}_2}^2 - 2r_{12}s_{\overline{x}_1}s_{\overline{x}_2}},$$

where

r_{12} = correlation between ratings of an attribute in Wave 1 and its ratings by the same respondents in Wave 2, pooled across all respondents.

In most cases, this correlation will be rather high, because there will not have been an opportunity for much change in many aspects of a product or service in a few months' time. Also, the same person will tend to give more similar ratings in both interviewing waves than would 2 different customers. Therefore, a high correlation between ratings in Wave 1 and Wave 2 will

• • • greatly *decrease* the size of the denominator, which will
• • • *increase* the Z ratio, so that
• • • a much smaller difference between means ($\overline{X}_1 - \overline{X}_2$) will be required for statistical significance.

For example, a difference from 8.5 to 8.7 in average ratings of At-tribute A from Wave 1 to Wave 2 (10-point scale) might not test sta-tistically significantly for 2 different samples of respondents. Howev-er, the same difference might well be statistically significant when ratings in each wave are performed by the same group of customers. Whether this latter difference is significant would depend on the amount or degree of correlation between waves, as well as the spread or dispersion of ratings on an attribute (i.e., the standard deviations). (The smaller this dispersion, the more likely that small differences in mean ratings will test significantly different, and conversely.) That is why the precise amount of difference that is required for statistical significance cannot be specified a priori when dealing with changes in ratings on some continuous scale.

Using Percentages

To this point, we have focused on using the means or medians of respondent ratings on continuous rating scales. This is usually most appropriate for numerical scales of 10 points or more that are properly designed to spread ratings along the scale. However, verbal scales often consist of fewer intervals (e.g., 4 or 5), and most ratings wind up in the top box or top 2 boxes. This makes it much more difficult to find statistically significant differences in means or medians from one interviewing wave to the next. In such cases, many companies prefer to use percentages, for example, percentage of ratings in the top box or top 2 boxes (e.g., 10, 9 and 10).

When percentages of this kind are used, the statistical significance of differences in ratings from one wave to the next can be determined by the Z-test for percentages, conceptually the same as that for means. There is often enough change in top-box percentages in successive waves to make it even easier to spot improvements than is the case with means and medians. Here again, interviewing the same respondents can increase measurement sensitivity, if it is possible.

COMPARISONS WITH COMPETITORS

When customers are asked to rate one or more competitors of the sponsoring company, there is always great interest in making comparisons in terms of attribute ratings, overall satisfaction measures, and "relationship" items (e.g., willingness to switch, recommend to others). This is especially true for purposes of benchmarking against the best competitor. The best competitor could be selected on the basis of survey ratings, or it could be a competitor who is generally considered to be world-class. The procedure for making these comparisons depends on whether a single competitor is selected (e.g., best in class) or if ratings are available for several competitors.

It is important to note that comparisons can be made either with or without testing the statistical significance of any differences that are found. In all of our discussions in this section, we assume that we are interested only in differences that are statistically significant, based on tests that are most appropriate for determining measurable confidence levels for any differences that are found.

Best in Class

Comparisons are much easier against a single competitor, usually the best in class. Note that this could refer to only a single company or a composite of ratings of several companies. This ranking can occur whenever respondents are allowed to indicate the company they consider the best of all the competitors, or it can be applied to the competitor that is rated highest in the survey. This can be performed for each attribute separately or for the single company that is rated highest overall. In either case, the appropriate statistical test is the same as the Z-test shown previously for testing differences from one wave to another (without the correlation factor).

RELIABILITY

No discussion of measurement would be complete without coverage of the related topics of reliability and validity. Every measuring scale must possess these characteristics if it is to be useful. Although different, these concepts are related in some ways, as we will see later. Briefly, *reliability* refers to the accuracy of measurement, or the *consistency* from one measurement to the next. Will the scale produce the same measure upon repeated applications, no matter who administers it? *Validity* refers to whether the scale is measuring what it is supposed to be measuring. Every scale must be both reasonably reliable *and* valid if it is to be useful for the purpose(s) for which it is intended.

Measurements in the *physical* sciences (e.g., physics, chemistry) are almost always very reliable, and usually are valid as well. Unfortunately, measures in the *social* sciences are much less precise. We may know exactly what we want to measure, but we have great difficulty in constructing measuring scales that are both reliable and valid to measure it. This applies to rating scales of all types, as well as to various psychological tests and measures and to different constructs in sociology and education. Therefore, we need ways to evaluate both the reliability and validity of any rating scales we might construct for CSM. Fortunately, psychometricians have developed good tools to measure both reliability and validity.

Measuring Reliability

Over the years, several methods have been devised for measuring the reliability of rating scales or mental tests of various kinds. These methods fall into 4 major categories:

1. *Split half:* the summed score from the first half of a test or rating scale is correlated with that for the second half. More often and better, the summed score from the odd-numbered items is correlated with that from the even-numbered items. These correlations should be quite high if the measuring instrument is reliable and if all items are supposed to be measuring the same basic idea.
2. *Parallel forms:* separate forms of the same types of items are developed and correlated against one another. The best example of this is the various written tests given to motorists applying for a driver's license renewal. Perhaps 6 to 8 different tests are prepared so that applicants who fail the first test can be tested again on a different but parallel test.
3. *Test–retest:* the same respondents are asked to rate the same company at 2 different points in time using the same rating scales. The second set of ratings should correlate highly with the first set if the rating scale is reliable.
4. *Cronbach's alpha:* a reliability coefficient that is based on a complete set of intercorrelations among all attributes in a questionnaire or test instrument. These should correlate highly if the scale is reliable (see Nunnally and Bernstein 1994).

All of these methods produce a "reliability coefficient": a single number that purports to indicate the accuracy of an entire measuring instrument, such as attribute ratings for CSM. These coefficients can be interpreted and considered correlation coefficients that can vary between ±1.0. We like to see reliability coefficients of upwards of .80, though .70 or greater is considered respectable. This would indicate that whatever is being measured is being measured reasonably accurately. However, we should never expect to find a reliability coefficient at or near 1.00 for customer satisfaction ratings (or for most other psychometric measures, for that matter).

An example of *test–retest* reliability measurement is shown in Table 9.1. It is especially interesting because it enables us to compare the reliability of human *physical* measurements with several *behavioral* measurements for the same group of subjects over time. (Unfortunately, similar measures are not available in published form for customer satisfaction research, to my knowledge.) All subjects were retested within 1 year from the original testing. Approximately 400 subjects were involved in this study, of which fewer than 100 were

Measure	Total		Men		Women	
	N	Retest correlation	N	Retest correlation	N	Retest correlation
Behavioral						
Keenness of eyesight (right)	415	.83	330	.83	85	.81
Keenness of eyesight (left)	414	.81	328	.82	86	.77
Snellen eye chart	241	.69	203	.69	38	.79
Highest audible tone	349	.28	284	.26	65	.43
Reaction time to sight	421	.21	332	.22	89	.11
Reaction time to sound	422	.24	333	.26	89	.15
Breath capacity	432	.89	341	.85	91	.77
Strength of squeeze (right)	431	.87	340	.82	91	.76
Strength of squeeze (left)	432	.82	340	.81	92	.46
Speed of blow	110	.51	96	.48	14	-.28
Physical						
Head length	433	.94	340	.93	93	.90
Head breadth	433	.97	340	.97	93	.94
Height	435	.98	342	.98	93	.98
Sitting height	431	.92	339	.92	92	.90
Height of knee[a]	230	.72	192	.70	38	.54
Armspan	435	.92	342	.88	93	.96

Measure	Total		Men		Women	
	N	Retest correlation	N	Retest correlation	N	Retest correlation
Length of middle finger	431	.96	338	.95	93	.96
Length of lower arm [b,c]	229	.98	191	.97	38	.98
Length of lower arm (right)[b]	202	.98	147	.97	55	.97
Length of lower arm (left)[b]	201	.98	147	.97	54	.97
Weight	437	.96	344	.96	93	.93

[a]Sole of foot to knee, while sitting.
[b]Distance, end of elbow to end of middle finger.
[c]Early subjects measured for one arm, later subjects for both arms.

Source: Johnson, Ronald C., Gerald E. McClearn, Sylvia Yuen, Craig T. Nagoshi, Frank M. Ahern, and Robert E. Cole (1985). "Galton's Data a Century Later," *American Psychologist*, (August), 875–83. © 1985, American Psychological Association. Reprinted with permission.

women. The same measuring device and approaches were used for both test and retest measurements.

As would be expected, physical measures are generally much more reliable than behavioral ones. Reliability coefficients for physical measures were all greater than .90, except for height of knee at .72 for the total sample, whereas behavioral measures ranged from .21 to .89 for the total sample. The overall pattern was similar for men and women. In particular, note the very low reliabilities for reaction times to sight and sound for the total sample, as well as for both men and women, and also for speed of blow. (These measures might be artificially low because of smaller sample sizes for females. The authors believe that some of the low reliabilities might be due to faulty measuring instruments and/or careless data recording by assistants who were gathering and recording the data.)

Whatever the reasons, test–retest reliability coefficients can show how accurate and consistent each measure is over time among a target population. Items with low reliabilities might be dropped altogether or perhaps reworded to make them less ambiguous. Of course, in ratings of customer satisfaction, it is always possible that the performance of a company or an employee actually changes dramatically from one time period to another, so that low test–retest reliability coefficients might indicate real change rather than unreliability. (To test this, a retest could be performed soon after the original ratings for a small sample of customers.) Reliability is especially important for measures of overall satisfaction, willingness to switch, willingness to recommend own supplier to others, and the like, because these are global measures.

In the context of CSM, test–retest and Cronbach's alpha coefficient are usually the most appropriate measures of reliability. A good textbook in psychometrics can explain in detail how to proceed (see Nunnally and Bernstein 1994). Every company should undertake to measure the reliability of its customer satisfaction attribute ratings to ensure that they are measuring reasonably accurately. The reason this is so important is that *ratings that are not reliable cannot be valid.* (This may or may not seem intuitive, but it is true. Measurements that are unreliable can be likened to measuring distance with a flexible rubber yardstick.) However, the converse is *not* true. A rating instrument can be perfectly reliable yet have little or no validity. Let us see what is meant by the term "validity."

VALIDITY

The term "valid" means that an instrument is measuring what it is intended to measure. Physical measurements such as height and weight can be measured very reliably (and they are also valid), but they may not relate in any meaningful way to mental abilities, success in high school or college, or various artistic or athletic achievements. Therefore, they are not valid measurements for these purposes or objectives. We need to ensure that customer satisfaction ratings are valid, as well as reliable.

Types of Validity

Unfortunately, the concept of validity is not a simple one because there are several different meanings of this term. There are at least 4 common meanings:

- • • *Concurrent validity:* accurate measurement of the current condition or state. Most physical measuring instruments have excellent concurrent validity (e.g., thermometers, weighing scales, oil dipsticks).
- • • *Predictive validity:* accurate prediction of some future event(s), such as success in academic or athletic achievement or future customer loyalty.
- • • *Face validity:* the measuring scales appear to be measuring what they are intended to measure.
- • • *Construct validity:* accurate measurement of some basic underlying idea or concept.

Actually, CSM involves all 4 types of validity. Ratings must accurately reflect how customers currently feel about various aspects of the company (concurrent validity). They should also enable us to predict future loyalty and customer retention (predictive validity). They must appear to be measuring factors or aspects that are meaningful and important to company management and employees (face validity). And they should accurately reflect the basic idea of "satisfaction" (construct validity). This is a tall order, and it means that some careful analysis should be performed in the early stages of constructing a measurement program.

In particular, concurrent validity can be checked by personal interviews with a sample of customers that has already rated the company or by comparing ratings with such factors as customer complaints, returned merchandise, hot-line calls, and the like. Predictive validity can be tested by correlating ratings with such measures of loyalty as likelihood of switching suppliers or companies, actual switching (from interviewing former customers), or willingness to recommend the company to others. These correlations will show how much of the variation in likelihood of switching (or actual switching) can be explained by any single attribute or by all attributes combined. If these correlations are low, it means that one or more key performance attribute is not being rated.

It is worth repeating the previous caveat that a measuring instrument cannot be valid unless it is reliable. More specifically, *reliability puts an upper limit on validity*. Loosely speaking, if a customer satisfaction questionnaire is only 50% reliable, it can be only approximately 50% valid. This is why it is so important for companies to test their own questionnaires periodically and to make every effort to improve both reliability and validity of the ratings gathered from customers and others on an ongoing basis.

REFERENCES

Finkleman, Daniel (1993), "Crossing the 'Zone of Indifference'," *Marketing Management*, 2 (3), 22–31.

Goodman, John A., Scott M. Broetzmann, and Colin Adamson (1992), "Ineffective—That's the Problem with Customer Satisfaction Surveys," *Quality Progress*, (May), 35–38.

Johnson, Ronald C., Gerald E. McClearn, Sylvia Yuen, Craig T. Nagoshi, Frank M. Ahern, and Robert E. Cole (1985), "Galton's Data a Century Later," *American Psychologist*, (August), 875–83.

Nunnally, Jum C. and Ira H. Bernstein (1994), *Psychometric Theory*, 3d ed. New York: McGraw-Hill, 264–65.

CHAPTER 10

CONSTRUCTING A CUSTOMER SATISFACTION INDEX

I n this chapter, we discuss various ways to construct a customer satisfaction index. Some of these approaches are very sound and produce results that are meaningful from both a managerial and a statistical standpoint. Others now in use make little sense and are actually misleading. The construction of a good customer satisfaction index is more complex and difficult than it might seem. We examine several possible approaches in enough detail to see the strengths and weaknesses of each. Specific topics include

- • • Steps in constructing an index,
- • • Selection of attributes,
- • • Weighting the attributes,
- • • Judgmental versus statistical weights, and
- • • The J.D. Power Customer Satisfaction Indexes.

This should help companies understand their options and enable them to design an index that best fits their needs.

Advantages of an Index

Results from customer satisfaction surveys can be analyzed at 2 levels: (1) individual attributes and (2) overall trends and comparisons. Thus far in this book, we have discussed mostly the former, focusing on the selection and measurement of performance on specific company attributes. This results in useful diagnostics that tell companies where improvements are most and least needed. At some point, however, it is almost inevitable that company management will want an *index* of overall company performance across all attributes rated or across some limited subset. Such an index can be useful in several ways:

• • • As an indicator that *summarizes performance* across attributes and produces a single measure of overall customer satisfaction;
• • • As a convenient way of *tracking trends* in overall company performance over time;
• • • As a means of *comparing the customer satisfaction* of different business units within the company, such as geographic areas, sales offices, and other separate administrative jurisdictions; and
• • • As a means of *comparing different companies* within the same industry (e.g., the J.D. Power Customer Satisfaction Index).

STEPS IN CONSTRUCTING AND USING AN INDEX

Several steps are required for a properly constructed customer satisfaction index: (1) selecting attributes to be included in the index, (2) selecting weights for each item, (3) building the index model, and (4) deciding how to use the index within the company. The process is not always in this sequence. Some companies might argue that Step 4 should be performed first, because the ways in which the index will be used could affect the way in which it should be constructed. Also, some approaches to building the index will combine Steps 2 and 3. Yet somehow, all of these steps must be carried out.

The discussion that follows in this chapter assumes that each company will construct its own customer satisfaction index. This can be performed either by the company in-house or for the company by an outside research supplier. The alternative is to use a *standardized index* of one kind or another. Some of these are available from outside *syndicated* suppliers (i.e., the supplier pays for the interviews and then sells the results to companies). Probably the most prominent of these is the automobile Customer Satisfaction Index by J.D. Power and Associates. This company also offers similar satisfaction indexes for telecommunications companies, airlines, credit cards, hotel chains, tires, and home builders. A similar index is provided by the Verity Group Inc. for home electronic products (e.g., television, personal computer, audio equipment). However, most companies will not have readily available indexes of this kind for their industry.

SELECTION OF ATTRIBUTES

Management always has a choice of attributes to be included in a customer satisfaction index. Management can decide to include all rated attributes, to use only a few key attributes, or to let statistical analysis decide this issue for it. Why would management decide not to use all attributes in an index? For one thing, some items will often overlap with other similar items being rated, so it would not be necessary to include both. Also, there is some merit to the idea of keeping the index simple with as few items as possible, which makes it easier to understand and work with for both management and employees. After all, there are probably only a few basic ideas that have to be executed properly in order to satisfy customers.

Another problem with using many attributes to construct an index is that if 12–15 or more attributes are measured continuously, no 1 or 2 of them can make much of a difference in changing the final index value. Thus, the scale will not be very sensitive to hard-won improvements by company employees. It will be very difficult to move the needle in the overall index, even though some items might have large weights compared with others. (This is simply a statistical artifact that occurs when too many items are added together and averaged, even if they are weighted differently.)

If it is decided that only a few items will be combined into an index, these items can be selected either by management, on a judgment basis, or by statistical analysis of customer ratings. Management can select a few attributes it believes are especially important, or on which it wishes to focus employees' attention, or that are considered keys to an internal quality improvement program. Or, it can let customers decide by finding the hot buttons using one or more of the techniques described in Chapters 3 through 5. As a general rule of thumb, the fewer attributes to be combined in an index, the more meaningful and sensitive the index will be.

WEIGHTING THE ATTRIBUTES

Regardless of how many there are, every item in an index must have a value or weight that reflects the relative importance of the item. Even if management elects not to weight attributes differently, the items still have weights (i.e., equal weights). The selection of weights can be specified by management or derived from the statistical analysis of customer ratings in a number of ways. Even if management elects to specify different weights, the outcome might not be what was intended. The proper weighting of items for a customer satisfaction index is usually more complex than it appears.

Judgmental Weights

If management elects to specify different weights for each item on a judgment basis, it will probably (or at least should) require meetings with supervisors at every level, as well as with affected employees, to arrive at a set of weights that is as acceptable as possible to everyone. When established, these weights cannot be changed without affecting the comparability of index values over time, so it is important to get them right from the start.

Equal Weights

If management decides not to assign differential item weights, then in effect, all items have equal weights. The overall index score for a given customer is determined by adding the ratings across all items and dividing the sum by the number of items to produce a simple average score. Then, an overall index for the total company can be produced by averaging these averages. This process gives the appearance that all items are weighted equally, as is intended by management.

But, this will be true only if all attributes have *equal dispersions* or *ranges* (i.e., standard deviations) of the actual ratings assigned by respondents. Because this is almost never the case in the real world, *items with greater dispersions of ratings will have more effect on the final index values than will those with smaller dispersions*. Thus, attributes will weight themselves in proportion to the dispersions or ranges of their actual ratings. An example will help illustrate.

Table 10.1 shows hypothetical distributions of ratings for 3 attributes from among 15 supposedly "equally weighted" attributes in a customer satisfaction survey. Attribute A has an equal number of ratings at each scale point, B has a much smaller (and more typical) range, and C has the most restricted dispersion. Which attribute will have the greatest effect on the final index score for the total company or any portion thereof? Attribute A, by far. Attribute C will have very little effect, because 80% of all ratings given were an 8. (At the extreme, if all ratings were an 8, the attribute would have absolutely no effect on the final overall index value.)

These are extreme examples, but they serve to illustrate the general principle that, in the absence of other differential weights as-

	Attribute		
Scale	A	B	C
10 Extremely satisfied	100	50	—
9	100	200	100
8	100	500	800
7	100	200	100
6	100	50	—
5	100	—	—
4	100	—	—
3	100	—	—
2	100	—	—
1 Not at all satisfied	100	—	—
	1000	1000	1000

signed by management, *items weight themselves* in proportion to the dispersions (ranges) of their distributions of ratings. Fortunately, there is an easy way of adjusting for this so that all items actually have equal effects on the final index score. The procedure is as follows:

1. For each attribute, both the mean and standard deviation of all ratings assigned by all respondents are calculated separately.
2. Each rating value assigned by a respondent is subtracted from the mean value of all ratings for that attribute.
3. This difference is divided by the standard deviation for that attribute, which indicates the distance (in standard deviation units) between the rating of a particular company or unit and the mean of all ratings for that attribute (either above or below).
4. These values are then summed across all attributes and divided by the number of attributes to get a final value for each area, division, or unit within the company.

This procedure is known as *standardizing*, and it produces a set of ratings for each attribute that has a mean value of 0 and a standard deviation of 1. These are referred to as "standard scores." In this way, all attributes have equal weights and, therefore, have the same effect on the final index value. A drawback, of course, is that all scores and averages are expressed in terms of strange decimal values that bear little relationship to rating scale point values or to the ratings actually assigned. This is a trade-off management will have to make if it wants truly equal weights for each attribute. However, the final index values can be converted to percentiles or grouped in some easy-to-understand way to make the process more palatable.

The reader may wonder why a company would want to give all attributes equal weight. Yet, one large supplier of an industrial product presently calculates final index values in exactly this way for all branches of the company (without standardizing). Moreover, the corporate office acknowledges that some of the 17 attributes are much more important than others (e.g., product quality versus getting promotional materials out on time), but they do not know which ones and do not want to change the way the index is calculated (to maintain comparability in trends over time). Furthermore, 6 of the 17 attributes are controlled by the corporate office, and not in any way by the regional people whose compensation is being based on the overall satisfaction index values. This company has struggled continuously, and will continue to struggle, with this system that was designed so carelessly many years ago.

Differential Weights

Alternatively, management may want to assign different weights for each attribute on the basis of its own judgment of the relative importance of the various factors. There could be several reasons for this; for example, management might want to

- • • Rely on its own experiences in dealing with customers over the years,
- • • Position the company in a certain way (e.g., friendliest, quickest) and assign weights to reflect this, or
- • • Focus on some past deficiencies on which it wants employees to improve.

Whatever the reasons, if it assigns judgment weights to raw, unstandardized ratings, these weights would be modified or even completely overridden by the differential effects of rating ranges or dispersions of the attributes, as was indicated previously. Therefore, the proper way to proceed is first to standardize all ratings and, only then, apply judgment weights to the resulting standard scores. This will ensure that all items will be weighted as management intended. The downside is that the resulting final satisfaction index scores will not be in terms of numbers that relate to original scale values or ratings. However, these can be converted into percentiles or standard scores of some kind that are more easily understood.

Statistical Weights

Most companies and research firms believe that a much better way to assign differential weights to attributes in an index is to base them on statistical analyses of actual customer ratings. In this way, it is *customers* who decide the relative importance of attributes, and not company management. However, the discussion that follows shows how difficult it can be to decide on the best set of weights for all items in an index, even after doing statistical analyses. (Incidentally, weights derived statistically will almost never be equal for all attributes, so this possibility will not be discussed.)

Each Attribute Separately

Chapters 3 through 5 show a dozen or more approaches that could be used to determine the relative importance of attributes for measuring customer satisfaction. Most of these produce a single value for each attribute that reflects its relative importance compared with the other attributes. For example, the following approaches all pro-duce a single numerical importance value for each item:

• • • Elicitation (number of times mentioned),
• • • Importance ratings (average ratings),
• • • Constant sum (average number of points assigned),
• • • Paired comparisons (scale values calculated),
• • • Importance correlations (r^2 values), and
• • • Conjoint analysis (utility values).

These numerical values (based on a single method) could be used as importance weights and applied to customer attribute ratings to produce a final index value. This is achieved by multiplying each rat-ing by its appropriate weight, summing the resulting values across all attributes, and dividing by the number of attributes. Here again, the proper way is to apply these importance weights to *standardized scores* and not to the raw ratings originally assigned by respondents. These weights could be applied to each customer's set of ratings, but they are probably more often applied to the average ratings for a spe-cific business unit of a company or organization (e.g., division, geo-graphic area) or to a company and its competitors separately.

Customer-based importance weights of this type are usually far better than management-based weights (from a philosophical stand-point at least), but they do have a major technical weakness. That is, these weights are derived for each attribute separately, and they tell us the relative importance of that attribute *without regard to all oth-*

ers. This presents a problem if scores for several attributes are added together to produce an overall satisfaction index value. If all items are completely independent of the others in terms of meaning, there is no problem. But in most customer satisfaction surveys, attributes are not completely independent, and in fact, they may overlap considerably. For example, several attributes related to the performance of salespeople or to technical aspects of a product and/or service are often included in the same index.

Combining Related Attributes

Whenever this happens, weights that are appropriate for each attribute separately are not appropriate for several *similar* attributes combined into a single overall index. The reason for this is that the same basic idea gets overweighted, and therefore overrepresented, in the final index value. One solution to this problem is to use only *unrelated items* in the overall index. These items can then be weighted by the individual values calculated by one of the methods in Chapters 3 through 5. This will produce an index that is free from distortion, and some companies will elect to do this.

However, the more attributes there are in an index, the more likely there will be some overlapping meanings among them. In this situation, the best approach is to apply *multiple regression* (or a similar technique) to all attributes in an index, whether 5 or 6, or 15–20. The multiple regression technique calculates a model that indicates the proper weights for each of the items when all of them are combined into a single index. In a model of this kind, when one item representing some basic idea is given a large weight, other items that represent the same basic idea get much lower weights to avoid overweighting.

Table 10.2 shows how multiple regression weights compare with simple correlations for each item separately for a study of fast-food chains (e.g., McDonald's, Burger King). Values in the first column (labeled "Simple r") are correlation values for each attribute separately, produced by correlating ratings for that attribute with overall satisfaction ratings, pooled across all respondents. Entries in the second column (labeled "Multiple R") are weights calculated by multiple regression for all attributes combined.[1] The same set of ratings from the same respondents was used for both calculations. There are several points of interest in these comparisons:

• • • Regression weights (beta coefficients) differ greatly from simple correlations (r values) for most attributes;

------

[1]These are beta (standardized) weights that are better for comparative purposes.

▼TABLE 10.2 COMPARISONS OF SIMPLE CORRELATION VERSUS MULTIPLE REGRESSION WEIGHTS FOR FAST-FOOD RESTAURANTS

Attribute	Simple r	Multiple R (Beta coefficients)
Their food really tastes good.	.53	.42
They have consistent quality in their food.	.38	.12
This is a place that I can trust.	.38	.08
They use high-quality ingredients in their food.	.36	.07
They have good value for your money.	.31	.12
I can always find something I like on the menu.	.30	−.02
The place is always neat and clean.	.30	.17
The employees are friendly and courteous.	.29	.07
The portions are adequate.	.27	.01
You can get quick service there.	.20	.02
The inside always look nice.	.19	.05
The buildings are attractive	.18	.002
The employees are neat and clean.	.14	−.02
The menu offers a wide variety of choices.	.14	.001
The food is cooked to order.	.13	−.08
I feel comfortable around the other customers.	.13	−.08
They offer new items occasionally.	.12	.03
The rest rooms are clean.	.11	.01
They never run out of menu items.	.10	.001
They often have special deals.	.08	−.01
They have plenty of parking.	.06	−.01
They are open long hours.	.06	−.05
There are many convenient locations.	.05	−.005

- • • The first item, "food really tastes good," has both the highest r value (.53) and the largest beta weight (.42); clearly, this item has the greatest impact on overall satisfaction;
- • • Other similar items dealing with food (e.g., consistent quality, high-quality ingredients) have high correlations (r values) but

much lower beta values to avoid overweighting the importance of food in the final index;

• • • This same pattern emerges in the case of "place is always neat and clean" (beta = .17) and "employees are neat and clean" (beta = −.02); and

• • • Many other near-zero or negative beta coefficients appear for the same reasons.

Which of these columns of possible weights is the "correct" one? This depends entirely on your objectives. The r values in Column 1 are the correct ones to indicate the relative importance of each individual attribute in influencing overall satisfaction, without regard to the other attributes that happen to be included in an overall index. However, the regression weights in Column 2 are the correct ones to use when combining ratings on all attributes into a final index value. Even though these weights look strange (especially the negative ones; see Mullet 1972, 1976) and do not accurately reflect the importance of each attribute in isolation, regression weights are derived in such a way that they result in the *best possible prediction of overall satisfaction ratings* for a total sample of respondents.[2] When these weights are developed on one sample (perhaps in a pretest), they can be applied to future samples of a similar nature.

Some readers might think, "Even though the regression weights in Column 2 are the correct ones for an overall satisfaction index, how can we use them when they are so misleading? The negative weights, as well as those near 0, will greatly confuse employees, who always want to know how much influence each attribute has on the final index value." There is no simple answer to this problem, but there are several options.

One option is to use fewer attributes, unrelated in meaning, in the index. Most companies do this by carrying out a factor analysis of a larger number of attributes (see Chapter 7), perhaps in a pretest. Each of the factors that emerges represents a basic underlying idea that several attributes have in common. Moreover, these factors are calculated in such a way that they are almost completely independent of one another. Then the computer can calculate a *factor score*, a single value that represents all the attributes in a factor in the proper proportion for each basic idea. All resulting factor scores can then be entered into a multiple regression calculation, and the resulting weights will almost never be negative or 0. Therefore, they will reveal the importance of each *basic idea* accurately, *and* they can be used to calculate final overall satisfaction index values.

---

[2]If all important regression assumptions are met.

Another option is as follows: When factor analysis has identified the basic ideas underlying a number of attributes, each of these ideas can be reduced to a *single sentence* that best represents the basic idea. Then, future respondents would rate only these single, relatively independent sentences, greatly reducing the required rating time. The resulting ratings would be weighted by regression coefficients, calculated in the usual manner.

Using actual (raw) ratings on the questionnaire scale as a basis, some analysts also calculate an average score for each respondent for the most important (i.e., highest loadings) items within each factor separately. This has the advantage of using numbers on the same scale as the original. However, these numbers will not be as completely independent as factor scores would be.[3] Even so, they would usually be independent enough for multiple regression.

However, if management wants to use 15–25 overlapping attributes and weight each of them individually, it has no correct way of choosing weights that both predict accurately *and* provide meaningful diagnostics so that company employees know the relative importance of each attribute. Probably the best that can be done is to use some calculated importance values for each separate attribute as weights, in spite of their statistical impropriety. At least employees will know which items are most important and have more confidence that the overall index values reflect reality. Fortunately, from a statistical standpoint, when more than 5 or 6 items are being combined, the weights assigned to each item matter less and less as the number of items grows larger. This means that the distortion in the final index value will usually not be great (but it will come closer to equal weights for all items as the number increases).

A Caveat

It is important to note that the preceding discussion assumes that all of the relationships between attributes and overall satisfaction measures, as well as among all attributes, are *linear* (i.e., straight-line). A good example of this is shown in Figure 8.2 in Chapter 8. Relationships of this kind are typical when simple performance ratings are plotted against overall evaluation measures, especially when these performance ratings are on a numerical, rather than a verbal, scale (see Figure 1.8 in Chapter 1). In these cases, multiple regression is appropriate to calculate weights.

---

[3]Comment by Gary Mullet, Gary Mullet & Associates

However, when nonlinear relationships are found (as in Figures 8.3 and 8.4 in Chapter 8), ordinary multiple regression is clearly inappropriate because it is based on the assumption that all relationships are linear. If this is not the case, there are several options, none of them simple:

- • • Use a variation of logit regression,
- • • Use dummy variables for each scale point,
- • • Find a suitable statistical transformation to apply to the attribute ratings that will result in linear relationships with overall satisfaction,
- • • Rescale the attribute ratings by substituting the mean overall evaluation rating for each scale point on a nonlinear scale,
- • • Calculate nonlinear correlation coefficients (e.g., eta), or
- • • Use other statistical techniques that do not require linear relationships.

Nonlinear relationships are especially likely when a single expectations/performance scale is used. Examples of 2 of these relationships are shown in Figures 8.3 and 8.4 in Chapter 8. In these cases, the ratings given by respondents cannot be multiplied by an appropriate weight calculated by multiple regression. Instead, each point on the scale is given a value that reflects its desirability, and these values are simply summed to produce a total score for each respondent and company rated. The resulting values are then averaged across all raters to produce a final score for each company, division, area, or office.

Choosing among the previous options is very difficult and will vary depending on the situation. It requires the services of someone trained in advanced statistical analysis.

J.D. POWER CUSTOMER SATISFACTION INDEXES

Probably the earliest syndicated customer satisfaction index is the one developed by J. David Power in the 1960s. It is certainly the best-known index today. Early on, there was only one index for a single product category: automobiles. (Today indexes are also available for several additional product and service categories, as was indicated at the beginning of this chapter.) Now that we have discussed alternative approaches to constructing an overall satisfaction index, let us see how J.D. Power and Associates constructs its own Customer Satisfaction Index for automobiles.

Actually, the company offers not one but several separate indexes for automobiles; these include overall customer satisfaction, satisfaction with the sales experience, initial product quality, and the new "Apeal" index. The general approach to constructing all indexes is as follows, using an initial, pilot sample of respondents:

- • • Do a factor analysis of all attribute ratings (they use performance ratings only);
- • • Select the 2–8 attributes that correlate (load) the highest on each factor;
- • • Construct a single composite factor score for each factor, using these selected statements;
- • • Enter these factor scores into a multiple regression model, which calculates the appropriate weights for each factor (because factor scores are independent, there are no problems of collinearity); and
- • • Apply these weights to future ratings whose factor scores are constructed using the proper weights as determined in the original sample.

For example, the Customer Satisfaction Index consists of 2 factor scores, 1 dealing with the car itself and the other with the dealership at which the car was purchased. The Sales Satisfaction Index has 3 components: (1) perceived salesperson performance, (2) delivery activities (e.g., introduction to people in the service department, explanation of vehicle operating characteristics), and (3) initial product condition (e.g., number of problems per 100 vehicles, interior and exterior clean and undamaged?).

Although the relative factor weights for each of these indexes are proprietary, we can be confident that they are market-based because they are calculated from customer ratings using factor analysis and multiple regression. This same general procedure can be followed by any company that wants to construct a customer satisfaction index using ratings from its own customers.

CONCLUSION

A customer satisfaction index can be very useful in summarizing ratings of many attributes. Such an index can be used in many ways, as was indicated previously. However, constructing an index that is accurate, fair, and sensitive is more difficult than it might seem. Management has many options in designing an index, but some options can lead to consequences that were not intended, as is indicated by some of the issues discussed in this chapter.

Usually, the best approach is to use attribute weights derived from a multiple regression of all attributes versus overall satisfaction ratings (or likelihood of switching, repurchase frequency, some other critical outcome variable, or some combination of these). This is probably the most widely used approach among large companies whose customer satisfaction systems were constructed by research professionals. It has the advantage that attribute weights are determined by customers, not by company management. Such an index can be constructed rather easily if relationships with overall satisfaction are linear, which they usually are in simple performance rating scales. However, single expectations/performance scales can present problems that require special kinds of analyses.

REFERENCES

Mullet, Gary M. (1972), "A Graphical Illustration of Simple (Total) and Partial Regression," *American Statistician*, 26 (December), 25–27.
—— (1976), "Why Regression Coefficients Have the Wrong Sign," *Journal of Quality Technology*, 8 (July), 121–26.

CHAPTER 11

DESIGNING AND ADMINISTERING THE CUSTOMER SATISFACTION PROGRAM

I n this chapter, we focus on several aspects of both the design and the ongoing administration of a customer satisfaction program. To this point, the book has covered mostly technical matters relating to various measurement issues. Although these are indeed important, if the overall program is not designed and/or administered on a professional level, all of the sophisticated measurement technology in the survey and analysis phases will not yield as much as it could and should. Here, we examine the following topics:

• • • Assigning administrative responsibility,
• • • Designing the program,
• • • Sample composition and sizes,
• • • Measuring customer loyalty,
• • • Relationship of loyalty to satisfaction,
• • • Reporting results,
• • • Ongoing administration, and
• • • Ownership of results.

All of these, plus other issues, clearly show why CSM programs are so complex and why they require continuous professional administration by knowledgeable and experienced personnel, both within and outside the firm.

ASSIGNING ADMINISTRATIVE RESPONSIBILITY

Any meaningful customer satisfaction program requires ongoing measurement of customers' attitudes and behavior over time. (In contrast, most custom market research consists of one-shot studies for specific planning needs.) This means that someone or some unit, either in or outside the company, must be responsible for overseeing the customer satisfaction program on a continuing basis.

Early on, many companies assigned this responsibility to the internal marketing research function because it was most knowledgeable about designing, fielding, and analyzing customer surveys. As time went on, however, more and more companies came to recognize the need for pulling the program out of the research department and placing it with a separate group of some kind. There were several reasons for this:

- • • Research analysts are already very busy with their own work and have little time for ongoing administrative burdens;
- • • Many (if not most) research analysts know little about the differences between conventional marketing research and CSM, as is discussed throughout this book;
- • • Customer satisfaction measurement usually requires greater precision in reporting results than most marketing research. The difference between an average overall rating of 8.7 and 8.6 can mean the loss of bonus money (sometimes a considerable amount) for all employees in a work unit or division, from the very top on down. This is not usually the case for most marketing research surveys;
- • • Many outside firms are available that specialize in CSM (some of these are separate divisions of conventional custom market research firms), and some companies want the confidence that comes from using experienced specialists; and
- • • Administration of a system or program requires more than just sending out quarterly reports. Company managers, as well as rank-and-file employees, need to know exactly how the system works, credibility needs to be built and maintained, complaints and questions from low-scoring units (the losers) must be answered, ongoing monitoring and quality control must be per-

formed to ensure the timeliness and accuracy of results, and so forth.

Many managers have come to believe that a customer satisfaction program is different from basic market research and that it should be administered by professionals who have the time and specialized knowledge to make it successful. Some companies set up a separate customer satisfaction unit or department within the firm, some place parts of the program in the hands of an outside specialist of some sort, and some do both of these things. In many companies, customer satisfaction surveys are given more attention in executive suites than almost any other market research. One reason is that the former often have a more immediate and direct effect on executive compensation and strategic planning than the latter. A program of this importance requires ongoing professional attention and administration.

Some companies combine the administration of the customer satisfaction program with that of a TQM program. It is a rare company of any size that has neither of these 2 programs, and most of the larger ones have both. Because both programs have similar overall objectives, it might make sense to house them in a single administrative unit. Some people believe that these concepts (satisfaction and quality) are very similar and can be combined within a single unit. Others believe that quality refers more to characteristics of the product and/or service, whereas satisfaction reflects the feelings of the customer, and therefore, separate programs are needed for each. Either way, they are different from conventional marketing research and require separate administration.

DESIGNING THE PROGRAM

One of the responsibilities of a customer satisfaction administrator is to develop the overall design of the entire program. For companies without a formal program, this requires a focus on every element, starting with an *original charter* from top management and ending with the release of customer survey results at periodic intervals, plus follow-up implementation efforts. Even programs already in place should be redesigned on occasion to accommodate new types of respondents (e.g., competitors' customers, former customers), better scaling or analytics, additional measures of customers' attitudes or behavior, effects on loyalty and the bottom line, and the like. A program of this complexity might require occasional "tinkering" as the company learns more about how to get the maximum value out of its customer satisfaction surveys.

Overall Design

Obviously, CSM programs are not "one size fits all." Although similarities will exist, programs (even in the same industry) will differ in terms of attributes rated, sample sizes and compositions, how indexes are calculated, implementation objectives, and even the overall objectives of the program. The objective throughout this book has been to present issues and options that should be considered in the design of any measurement program, not to present a single ideal format and approach. Designers should have read through this and other similar books *prior* to designing a system. In most cases, however, this is not done, because practice often precedes understanding and precision in many areas of the business world.

Legare (1996, p. 48), head of the Customer Satisfaction and Market Research Program for Hewlett-Packard's Patient Monitoring Division, points out the importance of careful up-front preparation before installing a satisfaction measurement system:

> Many attempts to use data for organizational change fail because the organization and the change agent have not adequately prepared for data collection and the events that follow. Without adequate preparation, it is not clear to people what data should be collected, what will be done with the data, and why they are being collected in the first place. Failure occurs because the necessary groundwork or contracting has not been done ahead of time.

He recommends clarifying the scope of the work, negotiating objectives, coping with "mixed motivations," identifying concerns about exposure and loss of contract, and deciding who will be involved with the program prior to designing the measurement system.

Another company that has given a considerable amount of careful thought to the overall design of its CSM program is Bellcore. Figure 11.1 shows how this company follows a "measurement development process" in designing satisfaction surveys for its constituent companies on request. Bellcore's view is that each of its client companies is different enough to warrant a customized measurement program, and it goes through the process shown in Figure 11.1 each time it is requested to design a CSM instrument and/or program (Brown and Devlin 1995).

Bellcore's process begins by assessing measurement requirements, including interviewing internal stockholders, cataloging the types of measures needed, identifying customer segments, and describing the services provided by the client company and its delivery processes. The next step is to catalog the requirements of the client's

▼ FIGURE 11.1 MEASUREMENT DEVELOPMENT PROCESS

Step	Activities
Assess measurement requirements	• Interview internal stakeholders to identify concerns and requirements. • Catalog types of measures needed. • Identify customer segments. • Describe the service and its delivery process.
Catalog customer requirements	• Use interviews/focus groups with customers to list service requirements (in their language), learn steps for obtaining service, and hypothesize dimensions of service quality.
Draft questionnaire and delivery plan	• Translate requirements into questionnaires, develop sampling plan, and select delivery method.
Test and evaluate	• Pretest questionnaires and make modifications. • Verify that questionnaires accurately reflect customers' feelings. • Evaluate whether questionnaires ask the right questions. • Determine service quality drivers empirically.
Field trial and set objectives	• Set service performance objectives. • Fine-tune reports and procedures. • Educate employees.
Implement and take action	• Analyze results, plan and evaluate actions. • Follow up with customers on results. • Reassess measures periodically.

Source: Brown, Marbue and Susan J. Devlin (1995), "Guidelines for Measuring Service Quality from the Customer's Perspective," *CASRO Annual Journal*, 67–72.

customers, using individual interviews and/or focus groups. Then a questionnaire is drafted, a sampling plan developed, and the type of interview determined (e.g., mail, telephone). All of this is pretested to ensure that questionnaires ask the right questions in the proper way. Next comes a field trial to set specific objectives and fine-tune reports and procedures. Finally, the survey is implemented, results analyzed, and implementation efforts evaluated.

Many companies will not be nearly this precise in developing their programs. However, a systematic process is the best way to cover all the bases and avoid constructing ongoing surveys without knowing exactly what management wants to accomplish with the measurement program. An approach of this general type makes it harder to get off-track and make some of the mistakes discussed previously in this book. Notice that the process begins with interviewing all the relevant stakeholders within the company that will be affected by and/or re-sponsible for the CSM program. Every company is different, and therefore, the characteristics of each program will be different. How-ever, something similar to the Bellcore process seems appropriate for use by most companies and other types of organizations.

SAMPLE COMPOSITION

Many customer satisfaction programs start by interviewing present customers only. They are the primary focus of the program, by defini-tion. However, it is not long before everyone involved wants to know how the company compares with its largest and/or best competitors. This might require a separate sample of competitors' customers. If the product and/or service category is one in which customers tend to deal with a single supplier at a time in a long-term relationship (e.g., in-dustrial equipment that lasts a long time, an automobile or truck), it may or may not be realistic to ask for ratings of other suppliers with whom the customer has done business in years past.

However, there are many product and/or service categories in which people or companies use multiple suppliers, or in which switch-ing is commonplace. This enables a customer to rate anywhere from 1 to 3 or 4 suppliers on the same set of attributes. The advantages are obvious. Results can be presented side-by-side for the company and all major competitors. Trends over time can also be presented for each, making the quarterly or semiannual report far more interesting and informative. Standards can also be set in terms of one or more competitors, or all combined, and the company can be compared with the best competitor on each attribute and overall. An example of this is shown in Table 11.1.

▶ **TABLE 11.1 CUSTOMER SATISFACTION RATINGS (15 ATTRIBUTES TRACKED)**

Mean Satisfaction Ratings	All Company Customers			All Competitor Customers			Company A Customers			Company B Customers		
	1994	1995	Jan-Mar 1996	1994	1995	Jan-Mar 1996	1994	1995	Jan-Mar 1996	1994	1995	Jan-Mar 1996
Attribute												
a.	7.9	8.2	8.2	8.3	8.5	8.2	8.5	8.1	8.0	7.8	8.0	8.1
b.	8.6	8.5	8.5	8.5	8.8	8.7	8.2	8.3	8.2	8.5	8.6	8.6
c.	8.5	8.6	8.5	8.5	8.9	8.7	8.4	8.5	8.4	8.5	8.4	8.4
e.	8.6	8.7	8.7	8.4	8.9	8.7	8.4	8.4	8.3	8.3	8.6	8.6
f.	8.4	8.5	8.5	8.7	8.9	8.7	8.6	8.6	8.5	8.6	8.7	8.7
g.	9.0	9.1	9.1	9.0	9.1	9.1	8.9	8.8	8.9	8.9	9.0	9.1
h.	8.3	8.2	8.2	8.1	8.6	8.5	7.9	8.0	8.2	8.2	8.5	8.5
j.	8.1	8.4	8.5	8.5	8.7	8.5	8.2	8.0	8.1	8.5	8.4	8.3
l.	8.4	8.6	8.5	8.5	8.7	8.3	8.3	8.3	8.3	8.5	8.3	8.3
m.	8.9	8.8	8.9	8.8	8.9	8.8	8.7	8.7	8.8	8.9	8.9	8.9
o.	9.0	9.0	9.0	8.6	9.1	9.0	8.5	8.5	8.6	8.6	9.0	9.0
p.	8.7	8.8	8.8	8.7	9.0	8.9	8.5	8.6	8.7	8.6	8.9	8.9
r.	8.8	9.0	9.0	8.8	9.1	9.1	8.7	8.6	8.6	8.6	9.0	9.1
s.	8.4	8.7	8.7	8.5	8.7	8.6	8.5	8.1	8.3	8.4	8.3	8.3
v.	8.6	8.8	8.7	9.0	8.8	8.6	8.3	8.3	8.3	8.5	8.2	8.2
Average Scores	8.5	8.7	8.7	8.6	8.8	8.7	8.4	8.4	8.4	8.5	8.5	8.6

Sample Sizes

In any survey research project, sample size is a problem. Customer satisfaction tracking studies have all the usual sampling problems, plus some that are endemic to these types of ongoing surveys. Some of these are especially acute in business-to-business applications. For example,

- • • Many companies, even large ones, have only a limited number of customers at any one time. How many times can each of these be surveyed in the course of a year without irritation?
- • • Are enough customers willing to participate to provide an adequate sample for analysis by region, sales office, salesperson, and so forth (for example, customers go out of business, do not return phone calls, refuse to participate, and the like)?
- • • What sample sizes are necessary to provide stable results for regional or office breakdowns? For small changes in rating averages or percentages from one period to the next?
- • • Business customers often vary widely in the amount or size of purchases. Should respondents be weighted by the amount of usage when calculating averages or percentages for each desired breakdown (e.g., total company, region, office)? If this is not done, smaller customers will often dominate within a random sample, because there are usually far more of them. Results can be very misleading.
- • • Is a single, central database available that contains all customer names, addresses, phone numbers, points of contact, and such to serve as a sampling frame[1] (rapidly expanding companies that acquire other companies often have a *severe* problem in this regard)?
- • • Who within a business firm or household should be interviewed? Is any one person knowledgeable about all attributes in the survey, or will it be necessary to interview 2 or more people?

These and related problems must be carefully considered and resolved before sample sizes can be determined. Every company and situation is different. Although some basic principles of good survey research almost always apply, every customer satisfaction survey must be customized to fit the needs and objectives of management in each product and/or service category.

---

[1]A *sampling frame* is a listing of all possible sampling units in a defined universe of respondents in which the company is interested.

Business-to-Business

As was mentioned previously, sampling is particularly difficult in the case of selling to other business firms. It is often the case that only a few large customers account for the bulk of total sales (the "80-20" principle). How do we draw a sample that properly represents these large customers?

One possibility is to draw a sample that is representative in terms of *sales volume* rather than *number* of business firms. Another is to separate out these largest firms in a 2-tiered approach. All of the largest customers would be interviewed (a census), whereas only a portion of middle-sized and smaller customers would be (a sample). It might be better to keep these 2 groups separate in the analysis phase so comparisons can be made. This also will enable a company to focus on its best customers by themselves, rather than folding them into the sample of smaller customers, in which they will be greatly outnumbered and, therefore, largely invisible.

CUSTOMER LOYALTY

Many companies these days are coming to believe that though customer *satisfaction* is very important, customer *loyalty* is even more so because it has a more direct effect on the bottom line. A Bain & Company study estimates that a decrease of 5% in the customer defection rate can boost profits by 25% to 95% (Jacob 1994, p. 216)! Therefore, most companies want to measure loyalty as accurately as possible and track it over time. There are 2 principal approaches to measuring customer loyalty: *attitudinal* and *behavioral*. Jacoby and Chestnut (1978) discuss both of these at length in their excellent book, *Brand Loyalty Measurement and Management*.

Attitudinal Measures

Attitudinal measures of loyalty are relatively easy to obtain. Questions addressing the following issues can be included in the ongoing customer satisfaction survey questionnaire:

- • • Intention to repurchase,
- • • Likelihood of switching to another supplier,[2]
- • • Price differential required to induce switching (cost per unit),

---

[2]It is important to make clear that there would be no price differential involved. Otherwise, some respondents will assume a lower price, and some will not.

• • • Willingness to recommend company to other firms,
• • • Willingness to "shop around" with competitors, and
• • • Comparison of overall satisfaction ratings for own company versus competitors' (the greater the difference, presumably the more/less likely to be disloyal).

Any one of these could be used alone, or a composite measure of some kind could be developed. For example, Burke Customer Satisfaction Associates defines a *secure customer* as someone who responds as follows on 3 questions: (1) "very satisfied" for overall satisfaction, (2) "definitely would buy" again, and (3) "definitely would recommend" to a friend or associate. They graphically depict a secure customer, as shown in Figure 11.2 (approximately 60% of their customers were secure). Another group is *favorable customers*, who give at least "second-best" responses on the 3 measures. *Vulnerable customers* give "third-best" responses, and *high-risk customers* (only 2%) give the lowest responses.

Using this taxonomy, Burke tested its own customer satisfaction clients in terms of *profitability* to Burke. Comparing the 3 best groups with the high-risk group, it found that vulnerable clients were 10% more profitable, favorable clients were 20% more profitable, and secure clients were 40% more profitable to Burke. We do not know if

▼ **FIGURE 11.2 THE SECURE CUSTOMER INDEX®**

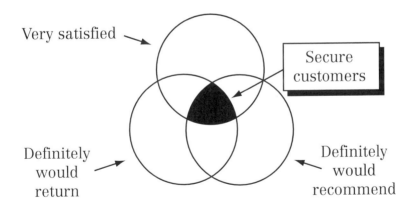

Very satisfied

Secure customers

Definitely would return

Definitely would recommend

Other customers are either favorable, vulnerable, or at risk

similar results would be obtained in other companies, of course, but an approach of this kind should be considered by every company with a formal satisfaction measurement program and a large number of business or individual customers. It is a way to link satisfaction to the bottom line, and that is always of interest to top management.

Behavioral Measures

Behavioral measures are even more powerful than attitudinal if they can be obtained in a meaningful way. Attitudinal measures of loyalty merely reflect what people *believe* they will or would do, whereas behavioral measures are based on what people actually *have done*. In product and/or service categories in which ample opportunity for switching exists or multiple suppliers are common (frequently purchased, many suppliers available, weak entry or exit barriers), respondents can be asked about the frequency and size of purchases from each of their major suppliers. Then, satisfaction ratings for each supplier can be compared to amounts purchased or share of purchases.

Another meaningful way is to conduct interviews with a sample of *former customers* that can be identified from company sales records or knowledgeable salespeople, using the same questionnaire as that for present customers. Any attributes that are rated significantly lower by former customers than by present customers (who have been customers for a reasonable period of time) are those that presumably have a measurable impact on loyalty—the greater the difference in score, the greater the influence on loyalty is. In this way, we can measure the relative importance of such attributes as price or value for the money, after-sale service, and product and/or service quality, as well as all other attributes. This is a much more direct measure of the determinants of loyalty than simply asking questions would be.

For example, if a company's present customers give an average rating of 8.5 to an attribute such as "always available for after-sale service," and if former customers give an average rating of 7.0 or even 6.5, this strongly suggests (but does not actually prove) that this is one of the attributes that drives customer loyalty. It should therefore probably be given high priority for improvement and training efforts. Conversely, if both present and former customers give average ratings of 8.0 to an attribute such as "attractive showrooms," it is unlikely that this attribute has any real effect on customer loyalty.

It could be argued that this is one of the most meaningful ways to determine which specific aspects of products and/or services really drive customer loyalty because it is based primarily on actual behavior rather than on stated attitudes or intentions. Of course, unavoidable defections (such as those due to movement out of trading area, bankruptcies, severe personal problems, business mergers) must be excluded from this type of analysis. If a company is more interested in customer loyalty than in customer satisfaction (and many companies are), conducting interviews with former customers is a very powerful way to identify these determinants.

CUSTOMER LOYALTY VERSUS CUSTOMER SATISFACTION

Because of the importance of customer loyalty, many companies track both measures over time, and most find a close relationship between them. But a very interesting study by Jones and Sasser (1995) shows that the shape of this relationship can vary widely from one industry to another. The authors visited several companies in 5 different industries and obtained their data for both satisfaction and loyalty measures. They plotted the 2 measures for companies in each industry separately. The results are shown in Figure 11.3.

At one extreme, local telephone companies can have extremely high customer loyalty, even with very low satisfaction scores. No sur-

▼FIGURE 11.3 HOW THE COMPETITIVE ENVIRONMENT AFFECTS THE
SATISFACTION-LOYALTY RELATIONSHIP

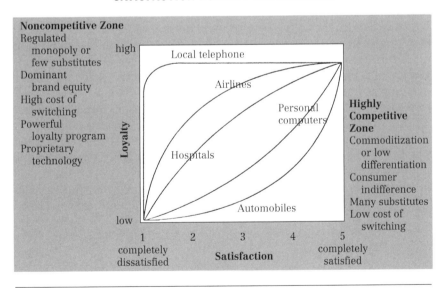

Source: Jones, Thomas O. and W. Earl Sasser Jr. (1995), "Why Satisfied Customers Defect," *Harvard Business Review*, 73 (November/December), 88–99. © 1995, President and Fellows of Harvard College. All rights reserved.

prise here, because most customers feel "locked-in" (though this is now changing as new options become available). Major airlines show somewhat similar patterns, perhaps because of lack of service by many competing airlines in some cities. In contrast, automobile brand loyalty is very sensitive to customer satisfaction; loyalty drops quickly as satisfaction decreases. Personal computers are more like automobiles, whereas hospitals behave more like airlines and are less sensitive to customer satisfaction.

Because these relationships vary so widely from one industry to another, and because of their vital importance, every company that is serious about its customer satisfaction program should *conduct its own investigation into the relationship between satisfaction and loyalty*. The preceding study suggests that some companies will have a much greater margin for error than others. Companies with smaller margins for error will be punished very quickly when customer satisfaction declines on an absolute, or even a relative, basis compared with that of competitors.

REPORTING RESULTS

Although results from all survey research need to be reported quickly, accurately, and clearly, there are some ways in which customer satisfaction surveys differ from most other types of market research. For example,

- • • Results from one or more previous surveys need to be reported in addition to current results in order to reveal trends over time;
- • • Results for major competitors should be shown also, whenever they are available;
- • • Accuracy is always important in reporting survey results, but customer satisfaction research requires extreme accuracy, especially when employee and executive compensation is involved. Even specific rules for rounding to averages or percentages need to be observed and explained; and
- • • If an overall customer satisfaction index is involved, the calculation procedures must be approved by management and explained to all involved.

Report Breakdowns

In some companies, top management wants results only at the total company level. More often, management wants one or more types of administrative breakdowns to show the performance of each unit for diagnostic and/or compensation purposes. How far should results be broken down? By area? By store or office? By individual salesperson? (In one extreme case, management wanted satisfaction scores for *each* of its approximately 7000 fast-food outlets in the United States. Needless to say, the required sample size was enormous.)

Obviously, the number and types of breakdowns that will be meaningful depend on the size of the total sample of customers and others that are interviewed. But this is starting at the wrong end. Instead of the number of possible breakdowns depending on the sample size, the sample size should be based on the number of breakdowns required by management for administrative purposes. This must be determined in advance as part of the overall design of the CSM program. Trade-offs may be necessary. Management often wants more breakdowns than it is willing to pay for. Also, in some cases, there may not be enough customers for an adequate sample in each breakdown (some companies must contact 5 to 10 customers to get 1 interview).

How many respondents are necessary for an accurate measure of customer satisfaction for any given customer group (e.g., sales office, type of customer, geographic area)? It comes as a surprise to many people that, (1) in general, for any desired level of accuracy, sample size does not depend on the *total number* of units (e.g., customers) in that office, area, or other division; it depends primarily on the *size of a sample itself* in terms of number of companies or people, and (2) there is no such thing as a minimum size required for accuracy. The only thing that can be said is that the larger the sample is, the greater the accuracy. This is hardly a surprise.

However, one fact that does surprise most people is that accuracy is *not* directly proportional to sample size; it is directly proportional to the *square* of sample size. This means that, to double the accuracy of a sample (i.e., cut the sampling error in half), we must increase the sample size 4 times (for example, from 50 to 200). This is expensive. Therefore, many companies elect to use rather small sample sizes for the smallest administrative units it wants to track. This often means 25 to 50 respondents per wave or reporting period. Any samples smaller than these could not be expected to be stable enough to reveal trends from one time period to another. Even these are not very stable. Of course, samples of 100 to 200 would be much better, but they also would be much more expensive, if they are possible at all.

Any good textbook in marketing research or statistics will contain formulas for calculating sampling errors for means or percentages, and from these, *confidence intervals* can be constructed. These books also should contain formulas for calculating the sample size required for any specified degree of accuracy or for any given differences to be statistically significant. However, as was pointed out previously (Chapter 9), differences from one survey wave to another of 0.1 rating scale units or 1 to 2 percentage points are not likely to be statistically significant *unless sample sizes are extremely large*. Few companies can afford this luxury.

In the absence of careful statistical analysis, a good rule of thumb would call for a minimum sample size of approximately 25 for any desired breakdown (e.g., sales region or office). Remember that, in order to double this accuracy (i.e., cut the sampling error in half), a sample of 100 customers would be required. If only a few breakdowns are needed, 100 or more respondents per unit would not seem excessive. But companies with dozens of units will have to do some serious thinking and calculating to arrive at sample sizes that balance accuracy against cost.

Revealing Ratings of Individual Customers

It is only natural that company sales and/or servicepeople will want to see the actual ratings given by those customers for whom they are directly responsible. This is especially true for the ratings of business-to-business customers that are the most dissatisfied. Salespeople and sales managers want to know who is spoiling their customer satisfaction ratings and why, and they usually request copies of questionnaires.

One large industrial supplier yielded to these entreaties from its salespeople and regional managers and provided names and copies of questionnaires for all respondents in the United States. The outcome could have been predicted. Salespeople contacted many customers who had given them lower ratings and contested these ratings verbally, over the phone or in person. Afterward, many of these same customers called the corporate office to complain that they were not told that their ratings (which they assumed were confidential) would be given to salespeople and that they insisted on, or expected, confidentiality. Some said they would refuse to participate in future surveys.

The same thing occurred in a new car dealership (Quirk 1996). A buyer was promised delivery of his car in 6 weeks. In the 7th week, he called the salesman to ask why the car had not been delivered. The salesman did not return that call or several others. When the salesman finally did call, he denied ever promising delivery in 6 weeks. Later, when the buyer was asked by a research firm to give satisfaction ratings, he stated that "the whole process had been unpleasant, what with the delivery delays, the unreturned phone calls, and the salesman's condescending attitude toward (the buyer's) wife." Soon, the buyer received a call from the irate salesman, who had been given a copy of the buyer's comments. He was angry and intimidating and would not let the buyer off the phone for several minutes. The author of the article states:

> When my friend finally hung up, he too was angry. He thought his answers to the survey were confidential and would be used for statistical purposes only. He was obviously wrong. When he called the dealership's sales manager to complain about how the information was used, the sales manager defended the practice and refused to apologize. Not surprisingly, he's vowed never to purchase another vehicle at the dealership. He also says he will never again participate in an automobile-related customer satisfaction study, no matter how legitimate. (p. 90)

Needless to say, this practice violates the basic premise of respondent confidentiality inherent in all professional survey research. In the absence of other information, respondents tend to assume that their answers will be held in confidence, even if they are not so informed. If a company intends to deliver these ratings to its own customer service people, it should clearly inform respondents of this before the interview begins. However, the company should consider carefully the effect this is likely to have on the ratings provided by customers. We could expect an upward bias in nearly every case. In general, the practice of providing identified customer ratings to involved company personnel should be avoided.

GAINING ACCEPTANCE

Let's face it. Customer satisfaction measurement programs are threatening to employees at all levels within a company, from top management on down. Even if ratings are not tied directly to compensation, employees cannot escape the realization that they are being held accountable by customers, as well as by their supervisors. This can produce apprehension and uncertainty, especially among employees and work units with lower ratings. Although there is no easy way to deal with these concerns, there are a number of actions that can be taken to soften the impact by promoting an understanding of the program and a sense of fairness.

The ultimate objective of most (all?) measurement programs is to make employees at all levels more responsive to customer needs and preferences. This can only be done *by driving the customer satisfaction program into every part of the organization*. There are many possible ways of doing this, as is discussed next, but they all require continuing efforts by administrative personnel, preferably those who have no other responsibilities (especially in larger companies). A program of this scope, complexity, and importance usually requires nothing less than a full-time administrator. Otherwise, survey results become a mere intellectual curiosity and little more.

Specific Activities

A large part of the task of administering the customer satisfaction program, once it is in place, involves such ongoing activities as explaining how the system works (e.g., sampling, index calculations, trends based on moving averages), its impact on compensation or other evaluative criteria, trouble-shooting, fielding complaints, quality control, deciding when and how to modify the measurement system, and reporting results to management and perhaps other subgroups. Early on, there can be a great deal of confusion, especially for the complex systems on which compensation is based. It is a very good idea to hold "information sessions" for everyone affected. And, a customer satisfaction manual should be prepared that includes a question and answer section.

Perhaps the key is *fairness*. If employees can see that careful thought went into the design of the system and that they are being rated on factors within their control, they are much more likely to accept the results. Here is where a careful pretest is helpful. Pretest results can show *why* the system is constructed the way it is and also that things have not been decided arbitrarily by management. Employees naturally want to know why certain attributes are rated while other possible items are not, how each attribute is weighted and why, exactly how an overall customer satisfaction index is calculated, how much improvement in ratings is necessary to move the overall index, how samples are drawn, and the like.

Ownership

One way to drive customer satisfaction into the company is to use it as a basis for changes in employee compensation, as was discussed previously. However, it has also been noted that employees should be judged only on attributes or functions over which they have control. This leads directly to the notion of "ownership" of the results by specific functional units in the firm. This is important because any well-constructed survey questionnaire will include a variety of attributes that refer to several different functional areas in the firm.

Therefore, each attribute should be traceable back to one or more units that actually provide the product or service being rated. It is important to ensure that people in each ownership unit understand what they are being rated on, how each attribute is to be interpreted, and exactly what needs to be done to show improvement. It is also important to establish ownership and know that people in each unit are motivated to improve. This might include offering special incentives for each unit that are tied to the particular functions for which the unit is responsible. Global incentives for an entire division or company cannot be expected to provide the motivation that tying rewards to specific controllable functions for each unit will.

In this way, each functional area knows the specific attributes or performances it "owns" and, therefore, is responsible for in the eyes of management. Some attributes are so broad that they refer to several functions or people within the firm (e.g., courteous employees, on-time delivery). Others are very specific in their references (e.g., courtesy of telephone order takers, responsive salespeople, pleasant delivery drivers). Obviously, the more specific the attribute rating, the more direct the linkage to a particular unit or person. In any event, tracing ownership for each attribute is a powerful way to drive the customer satisfaction program into every part of the company.

Here is an example from Total Research Corporation of Princeton, N.J. Its ownership planning assignments (Figure 11.4) link customer requirements (rows) with the functional areas in the firm needed to deliver each requirement. Geometric symbols indicate the strength of the relationship in terms of the extent to which each area is involved for each customer requirement. For example, "product reliability" is primarily the responsibility of engineering and manufacturing, whereas sales and technical support have only a moderate involvement. In contrast, all functional areas get involved to some extent in delivering good "sales support" and nearly all in "prompt delivery."

A chart of this kind can be very useful in explicating responsibilities of each of the major functional areas. Each area knows where it gets involved in serving the customer and to what extent. The customer satisfaction administrator can use such a chart as a basis for discussions with functional areas to establish explicit ownership. Also, low ratings on any major customer requirement can be traced back more easily to the people who must improve their performance in order to improve those ratings.

REFERENCES

Brown, Marbue and Susan J. Devlin (1995), "Guidelines for Measuring Service Quality from the Customer's Perspective," *CASRO Annual Journal*, 67–72.

Jacob, Rahul (1994), "Why Some Customers Are More Equal than Others," *Fortune*, 130 (6), 215–24.

FIGURE 11.4 OWNERSHIP PLANNING ASSIGNMENTS

Functional Area / Customer Requirements	Critical Needs Data: Importance Weight	Critical Needs Data: Competitive Gap	Relative Weight	Action Priority	Sales	Technical Support	Order Processing	Manufac-turing	Shipping	Engineering
Product reliability	31%	+10	+310		○	○		●		●
Sales support	22%	–5	–110	2	●	●	○	▲	▲	○
Prompt delivery	19%	–10	–190	1	●	▲	●	●	●	
Equipment features	12%	+5	+60		▲	▲		○		●
Technical support	8%	0	0		●	●				○
Flexible payment terms	6%	+10	+60		○					
Customer training	2%	–5	–10	3	●	●				○

Relationships:
● = Strong
○ = Moderate
▲ = Weak

Source: Adapted from Total Research Corporation.

Jacoby, Jacob and Robert W. Chestnut (1978), *Brand Loyalty Measurement and Management*. New York: John Wiley & Sons.

Jones, Thomas O. and W. Earl Sasser Jr. (1995), "Why Satisfied Customers Defect," *Harvard Business Review*, 73 (November/December), 88–99.

Legare, Thomas L. (1996), "Acting On Customer Feedback," *Marketing Research*, 8 (Spring), 47–51.

Quirk, Tom (1996), "This Satisfaction 'Research' Left the Customer Unsatisfied," *Quirk's Marketing Research Review*, 10 (October), 90.

INDEX

E

Elicitation, 46–47
Employee field reporting, 32
Employee surveys, 28, 33
Equal interval scale values of importance, 52
Equal weights, 183–85
Executive Order #12862, 5
Expectations
    deserved, 151
    expected, 150
    ideal, 150
    meeting, versus buying intention, 144–45
    minimum tolerable, 151
Expected expectations, 150
Extreme differences, 80–81

F

Face validity, 178
Factor analysis, 15, 107
    of supplier attributes, 108–10
Factor loadings, 108, 110
Factor score, 189
Fading attribute, 40
Favorable customers, 203
Final survey, 44
Fit with delivery method, 125
Focus groups, 15, 30
    in selecting survey attributes, 35
Frequency distributions, 15, 107, 135–37, 146

G

General Electric, 2, 3

H

Hewlett-Packard, 197
High-risk customers, 203
Hot buttons, xii

I

Ideal expectations, 150
Importance analysis, 107
Importance-performance gap, 21
Importance ratings, 47–50
Indifference level, 82–84
Indirect methods of measuring attribute importance, xii, 63–93
    choosing among methods, 91–93
    computer content analysis, 85–88
    conjoint analysis
        full profile, 71–74
        pairwise trade-offs, 74–78
    correlation/regression analysis, 66–71
    versus direct methods, 44–46
    extreme differences, 80–81
    indifference level, 82–84
    information display board, 84–85
    strategic cube analysis, 88–90
    subjective probabilities, 81–82
Information display board, 84–85
Intervals, 123–24
Interval scaling, 117, 118

J

Judgmental weights, 183–85

K

Key attributes, 40
Key Words in Context, 86

L

Laddering, 55–59
Latent attribute, 40
Likert scaling, 120–21
Linear relationships, 190
Loyalty index measure, 37